SOCIAL MEDIA
MARKETING
MASTERY 2020

————— ❧❧❧❧ —————

2 Books in 1 - How to Become a Top Instagram and Facebook Influencer with Personal Branding Strategies

Gary Loomer

Your Free Gift

As a way of saying thank you for your purchase, I wanted to offer you a free bonus e-book called **10 Easy Ways To Make $2k A Month Passively**

Download the free ebook here: https://www.subscribepage.com/business2k

What is passive income and how can it help you to quit your day job. Imagine going to sleep at night, and knowing that your bank accounts are filling up.

In this free guide, you'll discover what passive income and 10 lucrative strategies to earn $2k a month and more.

TABLE OF CONTENTS

FACEBOOK ADVERTISING

INSTAGRAM MARKETING

FACEBOOK ADVERTISING

———— ❧❧❧❧ ————

Marketing your social media to create a live business

Gary Loomer

TABLE OF CONTENTS

INTRODUCTION

Congratulations on purchasing *Facebook Advertising: Marketing your social media to create a live business.*

The following chapters will discuss:

- **Facebook Advertising 101**

  There are two billion people using Facebook every month which makes it one of the biggest and best platforms in the entire social media network for businesses and enterprises to advertise and promote their products and services to targeted audiences. Facebook Ads can turn out to be very beneficial for your business or enterprise because Facebook has 1.47 billion daily users and 2.23 billion monthly users; this allows businesses to laser target their favorable and profitable audience because everyone is on Facebook nowadays. Businesses can set crystal clear goals for the future while using Facebook Ads. Facebook Ads are a lot easier to keep track of. It makes it easy to trace the success rate of any ad campaign and it also makes it rather simple and easy to figure out the number of "sales and leads" derived completely from your Facebook ad campaign.

- **Facebook Advertising Strategies For Success**

  How are you going to "Define your goals"? In this section, we'll be shedding some light on advertisement strategies best for you and your audience. Once you understand why is it so essential to advertise on Facebook, The fundamentals of Facebook Ads and how they work, and even your return on your investment. Now you'll want to define your goals and objectives for advertising. Without a solid game plan, you will never achieve anything with your ads.

- **Facebook Pages and Facebook Groups**

  In this section, we have explained the concept and answered some questions about the key aspects of Facebook "Groups" and "Pages".

  - ***What Are Facebook Groups? What Is The Best Time to Advertise in Them?***

    The most interesting feature of Facebook is that it enables you to make groups and join groups. The social network has groups for everything, For Example, groups for dating, groups for buying and selling, groups for parenting, and countless more.

  - ***What Are Facebook Pages? What Is The Best Time To Advertise In Them?***

Pages that do not symbolize or represent an official cause or person are Known as Community pages, and these pages are keen to cover a long queue of things, from political drama to basic hustle, Usually, the thing or the product of discussion and entertainment embodied by such pages is something that is owned by an enterprise or individual or can't be easily claimed.

- **Optimizing Your Ads**

  How to understand the Analytics and Reports?

  In this section, we are going to explain thoroughly about the process of understanding and utilizing analytics and reports and answer question like

  - *How Often Should You Advertise? What is A/B Split Testing? What is Geo-Targeting?*

  The First thing you'll see when you open the "Facebook Insights analytics" tool is the "Dashboard" also known as the "Overview". When you look at the left sidebar, you'll notice a collection (list) of the many areas of Insights.

- **Creating Your First Ad Campaign**

  This section we are going to learn about Facebook Pixel, For example, What Is Facebook Pixel? How to Set It Up? Why You Need Facebook Pixel? We're going to go over everything you need to know about Facebook Pixel, including what you can do with it, how to install it, and tools that can make the process a little easier.

We hope you enjoy this book!

CHAPTER 1: WHY IS FACEBOOK ADVERTISING GOOD FOR YOUR BUSINESS

Facebook is the most known and used social media network in the world with 2 billion monthly active users.

Over the last decade, the world of digital marketing has changed remarkably altered. In the past decade, Facebook was originally designed as a way for college students to keep up with each other. But it soon grew to become a worldwide community to share news, pictures and more in one place. It doesn't matter where you are located throughout the world, you can get onto this network and connect with the people who matter most.

Why invest in Facebook Ads and how is it a reliable platform where you should invest your marketing dollars? If you are still unsure as to why you should hop on the Facebook Ads bandwagon, below are four key reasons why Facebook Ads can be a profitable asset for you and your business.

So Many People Are Already Using Facebook

Facebook is a widely used social media website and it has users from all parts of the globe. There are more than 2 billion people who use this social media site each year, and almost 1.5 billion of these users are on each day. This presents a huge market for your business, and Facebook Advertising gives you the tools to reach these customers.

Not only does Facebook provide you with a very large audience to advertise your business to, but this audience is extremely diverse. You can find almost any kind of customer you want on this platform. While 18 to 20 year-olds are the most prevalent users of this platform, the older demographics are growing as well. With the help of Facebook Advertising, you will be able to reach your customers, no matter who they are.

Target Your Ads Directly to Your Customers

Because of the large number of users available on Facebook, you get the benefit of being able to reach your customers, no matter who they are. And Facebook Advertising makes it easy for you to target your ads directly to your chosen customers.

Fortunately, Facebook commercials and advertising provides us with the ability to be able to target the customers to whom our ad will be in front of. Some targeting options you can use are:

- Interests and activities generated from what the user comments on, the apps she/he installed, shares, clicks on, as well as likes.

- Demographics that can be broken down by geographical, location, gender, age, etc.

- Main pages visited and viewed on your website (retargeting).

- Based on the activity on Facebook, you can use "Behaviors" you can also use 3rd organization partner information (data) from Datalogix, Acxiom, and Epsilon. The data involves device usage, purchase activity, and travel preferences.

- Records in your database of the subscribers' and/or purchasers' emails.

Facebook allows you to ask them for finding other related users, known as "Lookalike" audiences, something we will discuss in the following chapters after you have created an audience understanding and using the options I've given you.

Facebook's capability of collecting information based on the interests and concerns of the users, combined with their capability of targeting, makes Facebook an amazing option or method for advertising.

Set the Goals That Work Best for You

When it comes to working with Facebook Ads, there are two types that you can work with. Both of these are designed to help you achieve different goals, so you must make sure that you are fully aware of your goals before you get started.

The first type of Facebook Ad that you can create is an Engagement Ad. An Engagement Ad is when you want to have your customer take a specific action or interact with a post that you put up. This information can then be used to help you learn more about your customers, provide content to your customers, and make sure that you are providing the best customer experience to everyone. This Engagement Ad type is going to rely on the customers actually responding to your content and providing you with information to grow your business.

You can also work with the Direct Respond Ads. These are the best ads to go with when you want to use the campaign to generate more leads and sales for your business. These ads are specifically going to contain some kind of offer, along with a take action cue, in order to get the customer to respond. It could have a link to "sign up" "click here" or "call now". This call of action is important to make sure that your customer knows what you want them to do.

Before launching the ad campaign, first of all, decide what is the purpose of your ad campaign and then "Facebook's goal setting options" can be used to make sure that you complete that task/goal.

It is Easy to Track Your Facebook Ads

It is very important to track the success rate of each and every launched ad campaign. It is very important to estimate the number of sales and leads produced entirely from your Facebook ad campaign.

The process is similar to other ad networks and is simple.

The first step to set up "Facebook conversion tracking" is copying your particular tracking pixel and including that to each and each page of your site.

Once this is done, you'll have to choose from two options for "tracking conversions":

1. Using a web page "URL" you need to track custom conversions. For instance, you need to track sign-ups to a demo page; you will copy the URL of the page after the sign-up page and set Facebook to track that page (it would be a conversion).

2. Using Event codes for "Event tracking". This option is a little bit technical because what you'll need to do is to copy a little bit of JavaScript (just a line) and stick it at the end of the pixel code "(before the `</script>`)" on the webpage you need to trace. For instance, if you need to trace demo sign-ups, then you need to copy the "Lead Event code", that is "`fbq('track', 'Lead');`" Then you need to stick this code before the `</script>` of the pixel code on the "demo sign up thank you page".

If the steps mentioned above seem advanced and hard to understand, then there's another option, the code and directions can be e-mailed to the developer.

The Basics of Facebook Ads & How They Work

How Facebook Ads Work

There are many varieties of Facebook Ads, nowadays. You can use them to advertise your Pages, content on your Pages, the activity of users, and also your own website. Even though Facebook is growing their focus towards local ads and preserving traffic on its site, you can still be successful in sending users to your website.

Derived from the location, demographics, and profile info of users Facebook Ads are targeted. Only Facebook provides these particular options, no other platform cooperates this much. After your done creating an ad, you need to set a fixed "budget and bid" for every click on the ad or the first thousand impressions that your ad will gain.

Who Should Use Facebook Ads?

Just because some businesses are not a fit for "Facebook advertising" they fail dramatically. You should also keep in mind that you always have to carefully check latest marketing channels, particularly before the demand clouds up the prices, but also make sure that your business model is fit to work with the network.

Ads on Facebook seem more like "display ads" than "search ads". They can be utilized to produce demand, not actually to fulfill it. Facebook users are on Facebook because they want to connect with their friends, and relatives not for finding products to purchase.

Low-Friction Conversions

To be successful with Facebook Ads your business will want users to "sign up", rather than asking them to purchase your products or services. You need to use a "low-friction conversion" to succeed.

The traffic to your website was never seeking your product. They clicked your ad on a sudden impulse (action). If you depend upon the traffic to purchase something right away or to make your adverts ROI (return on investment) positive, you are going to completely fail.

Facebook users will carry on with their old habits on the platform, irrespective of you trying to convince them to buy your product or service. Rather, simple conversions are a lot easier to stick with for users such as signing up for your provided services, a short form to fill out, or Leaving behind an email address.

How to Target Facebook Ads

Marketers make a lot of mistakes whilst using Facebook Ads, the biggest and the most common mistake they make is not targeting the Ads properly.

On Facebook, targeted users can be listed by their:

- Location
- Gender

- Age
- Connections
- Interests
- Relationship Status
- Education
- Language
- Workplaces

Depending on your targeted audience, each option can be put into use. We recommend that marketers should prioritize concentrating on age, location, interests, and gender.

The "Location" enables you to target users in those countries, states, cities, or zip codes that you provide service to.

The base of "Age and gender" targeting will be on your current customers. For example, if women ranging from 25-44 are the majority of your customers (leads), then start off by only targeting them. If the results prove to be beneficial, Invest in expanding your targeting.

Return on Investment vs. Cost

Why is the Return on Investment so Important?

The return on investment is one of the performance measures that you can use. It can help you balance whether an idea is the best option for you. All endeavors that you take will cost some money to start. Your return on investment helps you to determine if the amount you spent is worth it. If you spend $10,000 on a campaign and you only bring in two customers, for example, then this was probably not a good return on investment.

To move your social media marketing campaign forward there is no single barometer that can guide you better than ROI (return on investment). Because you want to know about your Facebook marketing campaign results, For example, is it generating profit, leads and attracting paying customers? Is it worth the time and effort you put into it?

The formula for the return on investment: "ROI = (Gain from Investment - Cost of Investment) / Cost of Investment"

In this formula, "Gain from Investment" indicates about the gains and profits generated from the sales of the investment of interest. Because "ROI" is measured in percentage, we can easily compare it with returns (profits) from other investments, this allows you to measure various types of investments with other investments.

CHAPTER 2: DEFINING YOUR GOALS

Now that you know why you need to advertise on Facebook, The basics of Facebook Ads and how they work, and even your return on your investment. Now you want to define your goals and objectives for advertising. Without a solid game plan, you will not have the success with your ads that you want.

In this Chapter, I will teach you the various types of objectives you can set and achieve with your ads, and which specific types of ads are going to help you reach the goals you set.

(image 1)

The beautiful thing about the "Facebook Ads Manager" is that it pretty much lays out the potential objectives for each campaign for you. They even make recommendations on how to go about executing each of them.

As you can see from this screenshot (*image 1*) of the Facebook Manager, there are three main Categories, Awareness, Consideration and Conversion and then there are subcategories under each of the main headings. We are going to examine each of the subheadings in more detail.

Main Category: Awareness
Sub Category: Brand Awareness
Use This When: Your target audience are people who compliment and add value to your own business if you share their content.

You will want to focus on "brand awareness" as an objective if you want to help people find your website or Facebook page. These people generally are not acquainted with who you are and what you do just yet. This is your opportunity to set how often you want people to see your ad and visit your site, which is increasing brand awareness. Typically, you can choose anywhere from 1–90-day intervals for the ad reappearing in your target audiences newsfeed. You don't want them to see it too much or they are likely to tell Facebook to stop showing your ad. I'm sure you have done it a few times yourself?

Main Category: Awareness
Sub Category: Local Awareness

Use This When: You can only service a specific geographic location, you have a physical brick and mortar location, you need to increase sales or are having a grand opening.

This is an extremely useful objective if you are only focusing on certain states and/or cities. Maybe you don't sell online, but you have an actual store. For example, if you are a chiropractor or a restaurant owner. If you just opened, run an ad targeted at residents within a certain mile radius of your restaurant and let them know of your grand opening and specials! If you have multiple locations, you will need to make sure you have an ad for each separate location.

Main Category: Awareness
Sub Category: Reach
Use This When: You need to increase page likes, you want to get more engagement on your page and posts, or you are starting a new product line with new customers.

The reach is related to the number of people who could potentially see your ad. This is an ad you want to run when you cannot seem to get enough people to like your page, or you find that you just aren't getting the engagement and exposure that you want, in order to build authority and have conversations with your prospects.

Main Category: Consideration
Sub Category: Traffic
Use This When: You started a new vlog/blog, you have a new website design, and you launched a new product line or service.

This is pretty straightforward. Traffic means real people, not bots that you can buy on Fiverr.com from overseas. This is getting actual Facebook users to click on your ad and be taken to whatever landing page, site, or Facebook group/page (Which we will discuss later), you want. Facebook's design allows you to create a call to action button and the most commonly used one for people to be redirected is "Learn More". More traffic to your site ultimately boosts your Google ranking so you show up in search results sooner. Awesome, right?

Facebook Help has very clear instructions on how to set up a "Call-to-Action" Button so I shall not repeat them here.

To add it to your website, contact your web developer or simply choose one from the available options in your website editor.

Main Category: Consideration
Sub Category: Engagement
Use This When: You need to get some feedback on a specific topic, you have something noteworthy you want to gain a lot of views on,

and you have a need for dialogue among your page followers.

Page likes are essential. Do you remember when you were a kid, and we would all gravitate to the person who was liked the most? It's kind of the same concept. When you don't have likes or a lot of engagement, nobody wants to be the first one...so it's best if you create this ad to encourage it! You can get ultra-specific in this objective's settings about the type of engagement you want.

Main Category: Consideration
Sub Category: App Installs
Use This When: You need to introduce or get more downloads of a mobile app or a desktop app. You need more interaction with your app for revenue.

If you are a restaurant, or a consultant, or anyone that has a mobile app, this is the ultimate objective for you to monitor and pay attention to developing. This pushes the download of your app to the target audience you set. There are limited options about what it says, the default, is "Install Now", and that will take them to whatever app store your app is on. Be sure you have both an iPhone and Android app on each marketplace or you might lose customers right from the start. If you have a desktop app as well, you can push that in a different ad at a different interval.

Main Category: Consideration
Sub Category: Video Views
Use This When: You don't want to use video views until you have already established yourself as an authority with the brand awareness objective. You need an audience to engage with and take through your sales funnel by adding more value along the way.

If you haven't seen a Russell Brunson ad on Facebook, then you aren't on Facebook. This is the ultimate use of video that today's online marketers are using with the Video View ads. It has been proven, that video posts on Facebook get more engagement, and they are shared at least seven to eight times more than posts that don't have video.

Main Category: Consideration
Sub Category: Lead Generation
Use This When: If you get visitors but they don't take any action; you need to get new subscribers to your list

This is one of the things that most online marketers love most about Facebook Ads—the built-in lead generation functionality. This refers back to the Call to Action button feature you set up earlier. You have the ability to change what that text says. So make it count!

Main Category: Conversion
Sub Category: Conversions
Use This When: You have something to give in order to get an email address from your prospect but they have to go to your website or Facebook page first and they have to click on your call to action

The natural progression of a sale is: you establish yourself as an authority, your audience knows how you can help them, but they just aren't that sure how to justify the expense or just talk themselves out of actually getting the help they need. That's ultimately our jobs, right? To help a customer alleviate some problem? Whether it's time, health, money, hunger. So this ad is geared at taking those already familiar with you and converting them into paying customers and clients. If you are simply sending people to your website, you will want to make sure you have your Facebook Pixel's properly installed, which we talk about in Chapter 5.

Main Category: Conversion
Sub Category: Product Catalog Sales
Use This When: You have physical and tangible products in an online store; Holidays/Sales/Promotions; You want people to see your product features in more detail.

If you look at Microsoft, they have several products and suites, and software packages available. It is useful if you are able to do this as well. This allows you to feature multiple products within the same ad. You can set up a direct link for each product/service and even individual images. You are going to have to set up a catalog in the initial stages of your "Business Manager" Account setup prior to being able to run this ad.

Main Category: Conversion
Sub Category: Store Visits
Use This When: You have a brick and mortar storefront; you have multiple locations and you want to track individual store sales.

This is quite similar to the local awareness objective, but this adds a tracking element to the mix. It's on the phone! Yep! Your customers will access a real-time app with location enabled, and voila! You get real-time data every time someone enters your front doors.

Whew! Lot's of information so far. Let's keep going, we have a lot more to cover. So now that you have your objectives laid out, you need to move on to decide what ad format you will use. This can't be done until you have completed all of your objectives. It's the way the "Business Manager" is set up.

No matter if you sell candles or $5,000 computers, there is an ad format for your particular type of business. Facebook is great for the variety of categories. You might want to stick with one particular ad type without the help of a professional as combinations of the different formats have proven to be quite tricky, especially when just starting out.

There are five types of formats that you can use for your Facebook Ads. These include single video, slideshow, canvas, carousel, or a single image. Here is a breakdown of each of the ad formats. You will need to decide which one is best for you based on the objectives you have:

Carousel Ad Format

If you want to show more in one ad, this is the choice for you. This particular ad format is not only available on Facebook, but you can also use it on Instagram as well. You can feature 10 individual photos and/or videos and each can have a separate, clickable link. The idea is to tell a story with each product and image in the one ad. You can choose the order of each product you list, or you can let Facebook do it, using optimization techniques. Do not opt-in to this feature if you are trying to tell a chronological story with your products, otherwise, it will be random and not make much sense to those who view it.

Single Image Ad Format

This is a standard, one image ad with a standard format. A headline—a place for the description and the ability to add a link to an outside source.

Single Video Ad Format: Expert online marketers will use a single video ad to simply increase their engagement with their followers. Even though YouTube is a video site, Facebook has far outshined them as the leading video sharing platform. Crazy to think right?

The Slideshow Ad Format

Much like the carousel ad format, this type of ad format is just like what it says, it is a slideshow of static (still)images. These are a little quicker to load than video ads, so if you are dealing with a demographic or location that might not have high internet speeds, your best bet it is to choose this format not to discourage your audience.

The Canvas Ad Format

This is an exclusive mobile open type of ad. You can use

If you have ever used Canva before, this is quite similar you can add a variety of different formats like mp3, buttons, and even video. It is faster than even the slideshow to load and is great for building brand awareness. You can see examples on youtube. If you go to youtube and search for "Canvas Ads in Action".

Be sure that you sit down and establish your goals and objectives before you begin any other step in the advertising process. I suggest you start simply with the Awareness category and nothing else and then build on that as you get familiar with the platform and as a way to ultimately guide buyers through your sales funnel based on where they are in their buyer's journey.

Creating Your Funnel

Ultimately, the purpose of advertising on Facebook is to get conversions right? That requires a process or funnel that will help you convert those inquiries into customers. Facebook provides you with an advanced feature that allows you to get ultra-specific about your ad targeting. That makes getting in front of the RIGHT people, at the right time, extremely effortless.

No matter where your customer is in their buying journey, you can rest assured that there is an advanced feature that can help you to put your product and service in front of them at the right time.

According to Statista: "Facebook advertising revenue worldwide from 2009-2017 is $39.94 million U.S. dollars." That number is not going to go down any time soon, which means that as more and people get ahold of this information and take advantage of the advertising benefits, you are going to have to do more to stand out from the crowd. If you start off with a detailed plan and funnel then you will have no problems surviving the advertising world of Facebook.

One of the things marketers feel is the worst thing about Facebook Ads is that the ad performance is highly dependent on creativity and customization. They couldn't just use what they had been using or try to create a cookie-cutter ad with a one size fits all mentality. When in actuality, we come in all shapes, colors, sizes, backgrounds, etc. Literally.

Here are the specific steps you need to take to start creating your Facebook Ads funnel, but before you even consider starting a funnel, I recommend you identify who your target audience actually is. It is not often an overnight process. In the next section, I will cover how to identify your low hanging fruit, but for now, just know that the funnel starts with knowing who is buying your products and services.

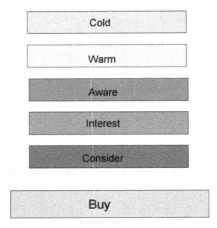

(image 2)

Step 1: Content Creation

As we mentioned, not every buyer is the same and not every buyer is at the same buying stage in their individual buying journey. You can learn more about the buyer journey from this article: https://blog.hubspot.com/sales/what-is-the-buyers-journey

The content you create in this initial step needs to be segmented. For example, if you are trying to go after chiropractors, lawyers, and dentists, each of those professions has their own set of routines, habits, needs and most importantly language or way of communicating with peers and others.

You aren't restricted to the types of content you share. In fact, it is best if you mix it up between videos, images, articles, blog posts, whitepapers, e-books, etc.

As long as it is most relevant to your audience and you remain consistent, then you are already off to a winning strategy.

Whatever you share on Facebook, be sure you are going to add it to your website as well, you will need to make sure you have it visible for Stage 4 and Stage 5 leads that come through your funnel.

Focus on helping them to solve a common problem or hit a specific pain point, or simply answer a question or break down a complicated topic in your field that nobody wants to touch.

It has to be engaging. You don't want to make the material so boring that people don't want to read it or actually absorb it. Using a variety of ways to deliver the content and keeping it entertaining and informative is a great way to provide valuable content on a consistent basis.

Step 2: Market to Your Warm List First:

Targeting people who have had some exposure to you and your brand is not only an opportunity to get new business, but it's great practice on what to change, what to strengthen and what to add or remove for your next campaign. If the audience that has some familiarity with your brand has a positive reaction to your ad, and you get some great engagement and posts then you know it's going to be ok when you get to Step 5, and targeting the "cold market" as well.

Step 3: "Look-a-like Audiences"

(image 3)

The term "Look-A-Like Audiences" began with Facebook marketing. Facebook has taken a lot of time to build up their artificial intelligence to be able to laser target on the customers you want to find. They are primarily used to reach out to new people who have not been in contact with you or your brand. They simply meet your criteria of low hanging fruit. You can narrow down how similar between 1 and 10 percent.

Step 4: Promote to Cold Leads

The same audience that you used to test out your ad, your "warm" market, you now want to take that content and expose it to your "cold" market. This will enable you to capture new leads and add them into your sales funnel.

Step 5: Re-Market and Catch Everyone

Facebook refers to this concept as "Custom Audiences". It simply means that when a person goes to your page or website and takes some form of action, they get coded, by whatever method you have installed, in order to track their buying behavior online. Here's an example. Have you ever bought something on Amazon and the next thing you know, you see ads for the same thing on the right panel inside of Facebook next to your newsfeed? That is what remarketing is. It is a way of simply reminding people what they are missing out on.

There are 3 types of remarketing that you can choose from:

App Activity, Website Traffic, Customer List and.

- **App Activity**: This handy feature lets you target your ads towards an audience based on how they interact with your app. Let's say they leave off of your site with items still in their cart. You can retarget them with ads that feature a nice discount or % off, and/or a similar product that is cheaper.

- **Website Traffic**: This is really cool. Let's say for example you sell camping gear. After you have placed your Facebook pixels on your website pages, then you can specify the audiences you want to see certain ads. So if someone searches for tents, you can expose them to ads related to the camping gear you sell.

- **Customer List**: This feature gives you the ability to load your own lead lists into the platform. This is similar to the upload contacts feature in LinkedIn. The messages can be customized and personalized and will target individuals who are a great fit for what you have to offer.

As we mentioned, you can't possibly begin to know any of this until you know who these people are, where they are hanging out and how to get in front of them on the largest social media platform in the world.

Who is Your Low Hanging Fruit?

Regardless of whether or not you have a big budget for ads, if you aren't reaching the right people, then it really doesn't matter how much money you set aside for advertising. You won't be successful. Nobody wants to advertise on Facebook without seeing an ROI, and it starts with who and the where. Who is buying your products and services and where do they hang out on Facebook.

If you don't know who your ideal customer or "low-hanging fruit" is, you can't provide content with value. That includes your ads. Not just your posts and blog posts. While demographics like where they live and what gender they are, are nice, they aren't enough in today's competitive marketplace to drill down and be specific to which you can help.

It just is not a strong enough call to action or desire, to guarantee any form of commitment or action on their part. There is no WIIFM moment. (What's in it for me). You need to sit down and figure that out for each of the audiences you serve. Here's what the benefit of doing so will do for your campaigns and how to get started mapping that out:

- Video, Written, Audio or Infographic: When you know exactly who your low hanging fruit is, you know what method of content that they will feel comfortable with. Giving them content they want, in the format they want it, is the number one way to conversion.

- Don't Waste Money: If you aren't targeting the right people, your ads aren't going to be successful, and the cost can add up pretty quickly, without seeing any return on your investment.

- The reason that ad blockers are so popular is that people are tired of seeing things that they don't find important at the time, or aren't relevant to them and their lifestyle. For example, a 70-year-old woman might not want ads for baby food. In a recent survey over 35% of online buyers want to be wowed and have a personal experience with the brands they buy from.

For these reasons, it is critical to evaluate what your target audience wants, as want will beat out need every single time. Look at where they are spending their time. What are they reading, what are they liking, what groups do they belong to, what stage of the buyer journey are they at, who are they following that is a heavy hitter in the game already and what organizations, clubs, and associations do they belong to?

This is going to require you to be a bit creative or you can hire someone to do this research for you. There are plenty of ways to scrape leads from the various social media sights and get insights about their behaviors. Once you know where they are, it's time to get your game face on. Get your content in front of them with Facebook Ads.

Each and every single one of us has a "why" for buying something. And it's not the same for any given two of us. Someone who you have spoken to on the phone and engaged with is not going to take as much convincing as someone who is just finding you through one of your ads for the first time.

Everyone has a specific level of information that they need in order to make an online buying decision. It's the nature of the jungle.

The key to surviving it is superior ads that take your buyer on their own journey allowing them to easily flow down your sales funnel. Do not use copyrighted images and videos, and be sure they are not low resolution. So let's talk about the other things that make up a good campaign.

What is a Good Campaign?

I'm going to use an example and break them down so you know what makes these great and see how the big boys do it. What you see is absolutely everything you can do with your "Business Manager Account" as well.

Paypal:

PayPal ✔
about 3 months ago

Where else can you sell online, accept payments, and manage your finances—all in one convenient place?

PayPal Business in a Box
Your all-access pass to running a better business.

WWW.PAYPAL.COM/BUSINESSINABOX

👍 21   💬 1   ↗ 1

(image 4)

Now while you may think that this looks pretty, well, dull, it does have its distinct advantages. PayPal is sending a simple and appealing visual. This Deep purple is said to be calming in nature and stand for greatness, majesty, affluence, I can go on and on, but I think you get the point. Using the color purple here is a great psychological play on PayPal's part. The color purple has been proven to stimulate creativity, calms your nerves and your brain activity, and evokes feelings of holiness. The Short Title is Under 5 Words or less and the subtitle is as descriptive as a paragraph. Nailed it!

If you're enjoying this book, I would appreciate it if you went to the place of purchase and left a short positive review. Thank you.

CHAPTER 3: FACEBOOK GROUPS EXPLAINED AND WHEN TO ADVERTISE IN THEM

Facebook's ability to create and join groups makes it an even more interesting platform. Countless Groups are on the social network for every purpose you can possibly imagine, For example, groups for dating, groups for buying and selling, groups for parents, and many others.

As we know, there are many Open groups on Facebook, but while open groups exist there are also Closed and Secret groups. In this chapter, we are going to cover all types of Facebook groups and how they are different from each other and we will also show you how to find closed and secret groups.

Now you must be wondering what is meant by "Open, Closed, and Secret" Facebook Groups?

The three types of Facebook groups are: "open, closed, and secret". All of these groups have some aspects and functions in common. The purpose of these groups is to allow users to share memories, organize events, and chat with their friends and relatives, although, some differences are there.

Open Groups

These types of groups as you can guess by the name are accessible to everyone on Facebook. It means that everybody is allowed to see the name of the group, location, members of the group, and posts within the group. The most important point is that everything that is posted (content) in the group is accessible in Facebook searches (navigation) and it is also present in the "news feed".

To join an Open Group, you don't need an invite or approval.

Closed Groups

By comparison, Closed Groups add some restrictions. Similar to Open groups, the name, description, and the member list of a Closed group are available to everyone. Closed groups' can also be found in "Facebook searches".

These groups are called Closed Groups for a reason, new members need to get approved by an admin or receive an invitation from a current member of the group. Moreover, only current members are able to see what the latest fuss is about in group posts and also in its news feed.

Secret Groups

Secret groups go by their name, as they are the completely private out of the three types of "Facebook groups". Nothing related to a secret group is visible to the public, only admins can add new members or they can be invited by current members of the groups to join, and only the members of the group are able to see posts in the group with or without comments. Although, members who have willingly left the group are still able to find the group in the search box and view its name, description, and location.

Visit "Facebook.com/Groups" and rush all over the immediate recommendations. This is Facebook's "Discover" feature for finding Groups for your interest.

At the beginning of the page, there are different niches for groups, such as, "Animals, Science and Tech, Neighborhood and Community, Arts, Travel", etc. Choose any niche to discover Groups both on international and local platforms.

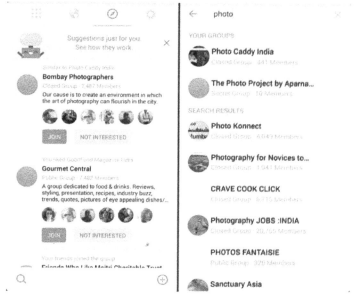

(image 5)

If you really want to go for it, you can start a group of your own, just know that is a long-term strategy.

As you interact in other groups you can encourage them also to join yours, never to leave a group.

It is not recommended to advertise in groups directly like in pages. Groups are rather used to build a "community and authority" that benefits you and your business by driving traffic to your personal pages and sites. Believe me, people will observe you for once, and if the entire content on your website, "your landing pages, are ready and dashing, all the links are working and you have a method to pick up calls and catch emails quickly", then you will surely hook them up at least into a chat or dialogue (the inquiry stage).

Facebook Pages Briefly Explained and When to Advertise in Them

A Facebook Page is going to be a profile that you make public. It can be used for a business, a brand, for celebrities, causes, and any other organization. Unlike your own personal profile page, these Facebook Pages are not going to concentrate on gaining "friends." Instead, you concentrate on "fans" or others who will choose to "like" your page.

Your page can have as many fans as you want. Larger companies could have many thousands of fans who want to follow them. This is different than a traditional Facebook personal page that has a cap at 5000 friends. These Pages will work similarly to your personal profile though. You can post updates, place links on the page, have events, and even upload videos and photos.

When you update your Facebook Page, this information will show up right on the page. Fans can choose to come to visit your page and see this information whenever they want. These posts will also show up on the news feeds of your fans if they liked your page.

On your page you're the master at the sail because you have the power to advertise as much and often as you like, you can guide others about advertising their businesses only on specified days of each week to get more and more interaction and page likes.

The most important thing in this chapter you need to keep in mind is that groups never allow you to laser target users (leads) with your ads. However, you can, do this by using a "Page" even if you don't own a website for your business.

Chapter 4: Understanding the Analytics and Reports

(image 6)

When you first open Facebook Insights, this is what you see—the dashboard (overview). To find the list of areas, look to the left sidebar of the Facebook Insights Features.

Take a quick look at these options:

- **Promotions**

  Giving " boost" to your post is how you can keep an eye on your promoted post and see how well they are performing. Depending on the goal you have, you can create a new promotion and there are a few options you will have.

- **Followers**

  If you need to find how many people are currently or new followers you have or how many have unfollowed you, this is to find that information.

- **Likes**

  To find the total likes you have for your page, paid ads or unpaid ads, who liked or unliked and the location of the like.

- **Reach**

  In this area, you can find how many likes, find who has reacted and the number of comments about your post, how many hides you have or how many Reports, the number of Spam and Likes your post has.

- **Page Views**

  To find which sections of your page are being viewed the most. A good idea would be to break down by Age, Gender City, and Country or you can use a device.

- **Page Previews**

Age and gender is a good way to find who has previews your page.

- **Action on Page**

To find what actions were performed or by who which device was used, the website or link the action came from or direction look under this option.

- **Post**

  To view your own post, not only yours and other pages you follow.

- **Events**

  If you're posting Events to your Business page, you will use this section to find the demographic and how has made a purchase.

- **Videos**

  Facebook Video Analytics, will show you the overall views of each video you posted. You can also find out how long the video was viewed in this section.

- **People**

  Get to know your audience, which demographics they are in or the language, when you look under the Page View and Page Preview tabs.

- **Messages**

  To find the number of conversation and your response time to people on messenger, also the percentage of messages that were blocked, deleted or marked as spam, look under this tab.

Ad frequency is not exact and you will notice that the "average number" is mentioned by Facebook. There's no real guarantee for anyone to reach for your ad to be seen, for example, a user can see your ad once and another may see it three times. Fortunately being exact isn't relevant and way an A/B Split Testing is important when advertising.

A/B Testing

Another type of testing you can work with is known as A/B testing. This is a strategy where you will release two versions of your ads, each having slight differences, to see which one the audience responds to better. The goal of this kind of testing is to make sure you are going with the right type of ad before putting a lot of money into a campaign. This testing could be used for a marketing email, advertising, web pages, and your business.

A good idea before making your holiday ads and launching is testing different content to target your audiences. Facebook Split Testing can be used in the Ads Manager or the Power Editor to accomplish a good ad. Launch sample videos and pictures ads, to control the formatting that will be seen and which ads are more appealing to customers. Test different actions to see which gets the most clicks, importantly you want to find how your loyal customers respond to each ad and which one is more appealing to them and which is more appealing to new customers

(Examples)

An ad can be viewed differently, to two different age groups, but if the ad is formatted correctly and testing is done correctly then both groups will get the idea of the ad.

Testing an image of a middle-aged woman, instead of a younger woman say in her twenties would not be perceived in the same way. So testing is important and worth trying before advertising. Even though A/B Testing is mainly common sense, it is important for an ad's demographic audience

As you start advertising on Facebook you will run into many things that you will want to test such as images, bidding methods, targeting audiences, campaign, etc. One of the mistakes newcomers make when advertising is wanting to test everything and have too many variables. Ex) This means too many ads and will be too time-consuming and will take weeks to conclude. When this occurs you are left with 2 options; Either create smaller ads with different variations or to use an external ad that is designed for A/B Testing.

After starting a new budget my suggestion would be to use a new managing tool to create new ads this will make your life easier and save you money and time

(Example)

An ad with a middle age couple would probably not work best when I make ads for my hairline better than a younger twenty-something-year-old group of friends out shopping at a hair store, versus a group of middle-aged women having tea and lunch, doesn't have anything to do with the hair business. So, learn how to keep a watchful eye out for trends and to relate to your audience.

Geo-Targeting

Geo-Targeting is a way to pin a certain audience for a specific geographic. It is one of the most direct ways to get your message across and have a very effective and powerful to boost your efficacy. With just a few clicks on Facebook, you have a new ad that's ready for advertising. But of course, there's a catch there is no easy route when conducting business. Taking this route can really jack up the price of your campaign.

Attracting higher value customers, businesses can benefit from this method whether it's a real estate company looking for a higher source or a B2B business looking to amplify a higher average, to attract new business that will pay more for the growth of the company.

Your business can use this method to help them find some new customers. You can place your physical location and then make advertisements to local customers. With regular outbound sales, this process could cost you thousands of dollars. But Facebook Ads can do the work for you without all the hassle.

In order to target the group that you want, you can just set up an ad with Facebook as usual. When you get to the audience, you can drop a pin in the area where you are located. This shows the program where you are located and that you want to reach other customers in the same area. After you have dropped the pin, make sure to work with the radius slider. This is going to let you pick how far away you want customers from this area.

So, if you want to reach customers that are within an hour of your location, you can move the slider bar to sixty miles out. This ensures that you get the best possible reach with this feature.

Seasonal Ad Campaigns for an extra boost

Facebook marketers have an array of tools to rely on for help generate leads, there are a few big ones that we need to take a look at.

Targeting Options

Though you can target users using the location, age, Gender or interests to find out people who like your page or app, by searching families or certain people within a household to target a specific ad. You will be able to do this by uploading your own audience, to similar people of your already targeted audiences.

Facebook's Cross-Border Insights Finder to compare data between the use of International Customers to compare data and unlock opportunities.

You can target specific shoppers for the holidays between Thanksgiving and New Year's Day. Facebook identifies holiday shoppers, by the specific post about Black Friday and Cyber Monday and keep in mind that you aren't just targeting shoppers who are only buying gifts but those who are also looking for something for themselves. Self-gifting is becoming quite popular according to a Facebook survey, of course, if you're having trouble finding an audience start with your target.

Another suggestion Facebook recommendation is to go through your customer database to better understand your audience and demographics of past holiday history to reach those buyers again or new buyers.

Use the Facebook Audience Insights tool, to better understand customers and purchase behavior if you haven't already launched a new ad. Using this information you can effectively target users and creating ads that will be more appealing to customers and potential customers.

Facebook users are now making more purchases using their mobiles. 61% of shoppers between Black Friday and Cyber Monday are found to be males using Facebook. Facebook holiday shoppers are known to use their mobile more during the holiday, to receive free gifts with their purchase.

People are known to use their smartphones in stores to compare prices, compare products, take photos re-review and get discounts. Consumers will have plenty of choices when making their holiday purchases.

CHAPTER 5: CREATING YOUR FIRST AD CAMPAIGN

N ow it is time to go through and create your very first ad campaign. This process is pretty simple to do. And once you complete the process one time, you will be able to go through it over and over again and it will only take a few minutes to complete. Make sure that you have information about your target audience, a good idea of your budget, and more in place ahead of time to make sure you can speed up the process.

Facebook Pixel Explained & How to Set It Up

There are two distinct Facebook pixels; the conversation pixel, and the tracking audience. Facebook combined these 2 one upgrade tracking pixel. In this section, everything you need to know about Facebook pixel will be discussed, including how to install it, how you can do it, and tools that can make the process easier.Why would you need Facebook pixels? Facebook's tracking pixel has two major capabilities to track users who took action because of your Facebook ad and to track activity on your site. If you're running Facebook Ads, you should install the pixel.

Let's look at the first purpose: alone this is worthy of installing pixel because of measuring the licks to your site, (you'll actually be able to see your users' actions, that maybe signing up or making a purchase.) You'll actually be paying for the conversion. If you aren't getting the results you want, troubleshoot your ads more effectively: you know that the ad is great but something isn't quite cutting it for your customers. Due to specific action on your site (like visiting certain pages or not complete their purchase), it can help you target messages to warm audiences., making your ad more relevant, lowering your relevance score and saving you money.

To find your tracking pixel ads each Facebook account gets one-pixel which you'll install on every page, but different from the old tracking pixel where you would have to install the different types of tracking pixels for each image (conversation, one for views, etc.) on each page.

Accessing Your Tracking Pixel Through Your Ads Manager

When "creating pixel" just names the order to create the new pixel. You will see a note after signing up for a business manager and have the options.

Set up Facebook Pixel

Install your pixel code   ×

To use the Facebook pixel, you must first install the pixel code on your website. This code sends site visit information back to Facebook so that you can measure customer actions and create smarter advertising.

Choose an option to install the pixel code. You can change this choice later.

Use an integration or tag manager
The Facebook pixel can currently be integrated with BigCommerce, Google Tag Manager, Magento, Segment, Shopify, Squarespace, Wix, WooCommerce and many more. Learn about platform integrations.

Manually install the code yourself
We'll walk you through the steps to install the pixel code.

Email instructions to a developer
Send the installation instructions to a developer so that they can install the pixel code for you.

Cancel

(image 7)

From here, you can make a few choices for how to install and use your Facebook Pixel tool. The options you can choose from include:

- Get some instructions emailed to you from the developer

- Install the code manually. You will need to know some coding to do this method.

- Use what is known as a tag or integration manager.

54

At this point, you need to click on the button for "Use an integration or tag manager. This allows you to see if Facebook was able to match up with your website platform. If you see that your site builder is listed there, you are in luck. The rest of the setup for Pixel is going to be really simple.

Look for your platform and then follow the instructions that come up on the screen.

There are times when your website builder won't be listed on the menu. You may also not have a developer who can send you the instructions. When this happens, you will need to go through and manually install the pixel. The steps that you need to do this include:

Click on "Manually install the code yourself".

Look through the new menu. It is going to show you the next three steps you can follow. The steps are going to vary based on the computer system you use.

You will be able to see the code you need for Facebook Pixel as the second step. This is the base code and you need to install it on each page of your website to make it work properly. The platform that you use for your business website is going to determine how many more steps you will need to use.

Many people use WordPress to create their business websites. This platform is nice to work with because its free plugin, known as PixelYourSite, will make it easy to install this program on each page of the website, and you only need to push one button.

NOTE: If you are using another platform besides WordPress, you will need to find the instructions for that site. This is going on the presumption your website is in WordPress.

Go to the plugins menu and search for PixelYourSite.

Click install.

Activate the Pixel

Installing Plugin: Facebook Pixel by PixelYourSite - Standard Events & WooCommerce 3.1.0

Downloading install package from https://downloads.wordpress.org/plugin/pixelyoursite.3.1.0.zip...

Unpacking the package...

Installing the plugin...

Successfully installed the plugin Facebook Pixel by PixelYourSite - Standard Events & WooCommerce 3.1.0.

Activate Plugin | Return to Plugin Installer

Some of your translations need updating. Sit tight for a few more seconds while we update them as well.

Updating translations for Akismet (en_GB)...

Translation updated successfully.

(image 8)

After this plugin has been installed and you have time to activate it, you should go to the dashboard for PixelYourSite. Here you need to take the Pixel ID and enter it into the right section. If you are not sure what your Pixel ID is, you should go back to the manager for your Facebook Ads. There is a Pixels tab there on the top corner under the name of your Pixel. Copy that number and then paste it into the dashboard.

After the Pixel ID is in place, scroll to the bottom of the screen so that you can Save Settings.

After you finish these steps, you will have Facebook pixel installed on your site. The next time someone comes to your website, whether they get there from email, search, or social media, they will be tagged by that pixel and matched up on Facebook. This helps you to build up the custom audience based on the people who have visited that site.

How to Check If the Pixel Program Is Working

The next thing to do is make sure that the Pixel program is working. To do this, you need to head back to your website and let a page load up. From here, you can go back to your Pixels tab, which is back in the Ads manager. There should be a green dot there that will say when your pixel was last active. It should have the time when you last loaded a page of your website.

Now that you took the time to create one of these Pixels and it is installed on your site, you can now take that information and build up a custom audience. This custom audience is going to include demographics of those who have actually visited your website.

To create this custom audience, you can go back to the Ads Manager and click on "Pixels" again. In the dashboard, you can click on "Create Custom Audience. You will see a pop up that appears that says something similar to "Create custom website audience."

For now, we are going to work on a custom audience, but will try to keep it simple. We are just going to create an audience out of everyone who has visited your site. Make sure that you select the Pixel and that you see a green dot there. This means that it is active. You can also keep the "all website visitors" part clicked. Take a look at how many days are in the field. You can pick between 30 to 180 days depending on your needs. A good rule of thumb here is that when you are doing a retargeting campaign, the more days from when someone last came to your site, the lower CTR you will have. Make sure to give this audience a name so you can remember it.

After this information is set up, you can click on create an audience. There will be a new message that comes up that alerts you that this audience is created. You can always check on that new audience with your Audience tab, located right next to the Pixel tab we used earlier.

Facebook Ads Manager

The next thing that we are going to look at is Facebook Ads Manager. This is free for you to use. Facebook asks that you set up a campaign with the help of Ads Manager though (we do not suggest that you use Power Editor because it is the more complex tool. You would not want to use this method because it is used by agencies and enterprise- level advertisers.) When using the Facebook Ads Manager you can:

Ad sets and new ads can be created Facebook ad bids can be managed

Different audiences can be targeted

Ad campaigns can be optimized

Campaign performances keep track

Facebook ad campaigns can be a/b

Facebook Ads Manager accounts have 3 ways to be Access: bookmark the link for quick access, click on the drop-down arrow that can be found in the upper right corner and "Manage Ads" located in the drop- down menu however

However, Facebook suggests playing around with the Ads Manager to see what you would find.

When you get to this step, you will want to click on the Facebook Business Manager. From here, you can gain access to a lot of useful information. You can see information about all your reports, your audience on Facebook, and more. You will want to check out this part of your Facebook Ads account.

Some people make the misconception that budget is all that matters. Now you're asking for trouble to approach you and very quickly I might add! Instead, you should check that the results you get is worth what you are spending on that campaign (ex) $69 per bundle -$35 but It's up to you to decide if that's worth it or not for your business or just wasting as space. A number of results you are getting are also an important factor. If you are going to put a lot of money and your time into an ad campaign, and you don't get a lot of results out of that campaign, if you're putting time and energy into them and running campaigns, while only getting little results, you may want to consider opting to a different platform or trying new strategies.

People should see your ad a few times before they decide to purchase with you, but if you get 0 to 3 likes, it is safe to say that no one is shopping with you. And over time your relevance score will be affected, you will want to keep a close eye on how active your campaigns and if the frequency keeps getting too high.

You do need to monitor this information, but you don't have to stress out about it as much as the other two options. There is some really important information that comes into play here that can really benefit you. For example, it is going to help you break down information about your target audience into fields like:

- Location
- Age
- Gender
- Other pages they like
- The interests that they show on Facebook
- Household information, if Facebook has it.

Knowing information about your target audience is very important, and seeing whether the target audience is changing or not can make a big difference in your future marketing endeavors. But it is not really going to show you how effective the advertising is doing. Check on it occasionally, but focus on the other metrics more.

You can view your target audiences, using this data. You might end up getting fresh concepts for new campaigns to run. I personally make campaigns that are aimed directly at customers who I know likes a specific topic and get surprisingly strong feedback.

Because Facebook users spend a considerable amount of time on the social network as a way to be entertained and spend time, unlike Google, where they go for a specific reason (to search for something), Facebook is a far more social environment. And with that social aspect, comes an opportunity for brands to grab the attention of their target audience.

Of course, simply advertising on Facebook isn't enough. You need to know how to create, launch, and analyze that ad so that you can optimize your campaign and increase your ROI for future campaigns.

Creating Your First Live Ad

"How can you start creating a new Facebook campaign?"
To answer this question, let's start with the basics.

You'll be given prompt directions the entire campaign creation funnel (image below). Just put in a few ad details like images and copy for a new ad to be created.

Step 1: Select Your Campaign Objective

In this step, you can choose from some of the options below to help you pick out the right campaign objective.

- Local awareness or reaching customers near you.
- How far you want the reach to go
- Brand awareness
- Lead generation
- Traffic
- Video views and if the video is going viral
- Conversions
- How many customers visit your store
- All installs.

Step 2: Name Your Campaign

Naming your campaign is the next step. This is important because it can help you to keep things organized. No one else is going to see the name of this campaign, so you can pick any name that you want. But pick something that will be easy for you to remember and keep track of. The name tells it all, so you want to be as creative as possible. When you pick out a name for your ad, make sure that you add the date in there somehow. This can be helpful in the future when you want to look back at it and you are trying to find it among a list of other campaigns.

Step 3: Finding the Target Audience

The next step is to pick out your target audience. You can choose to make a new custom audience or you can work with one of your current saved audience. Make sure you take some time to pick out a good target audience. You can easily have a fantastic campaign, but if you are not targeting it to the right people, you won't get any results.

Step 4: How to Set Up Ad Placement

There are several different places where you are able to put your Facebook Ads. The right location can make all the difference in whether your potential customers will actually see the ads or not. Some of the options you have for ad placement include:

- Audience network
- News Feeds
- Instant articles
- In-stream video
- Instagram

When you are setting up a campaign, you can choose to either let the Facebook program do the placement, through Automatic Placement, or you can go through and configure the campaign manually. Facebook often does a good job with ad placements. If you have data that shows another placement would provide you with a better return on investment than what Facebook is proposing, then it may be best to do this part manually. For your first campaign, consider using Automatic Placements to make things easier. The information you glean from this first campaign can be used to help you with making manual campaigns later on.

Step 5: How to Pick Your Budget for Your Campaign

Now it is time to set up the budget for your campaign and begin bidding. Picking the right budget for your project is going to be very important when it comes to how successful the campaign will be. You don't want to put a budget that is too small, or you won't reach the customers that you want. But if you place a budget that is too large, you could waste a lot of money.

When you work with Facebook, you can pick from two main budgeting options. The first option is a daily budget. This is the amount that you authorize Facebook to spend when they deliver your ads each day of the campaign. When you set this daily budget, you are telling Facebook to get you as many results as they can for the budget you pick.

There are times when Facebook will spend more than what you set for the daily budget. But it will even out to give you the average that you set. For example, if Facebook sees that there is a day or two with high-potential for your campaign; it could decide to spend more than you set for the daily budget. This won't go more than 25 percent above that daily budget. Then on days that Facebook sees as low potential, the program will spend less than your budget.

As you look through your daily budget, it is likely that your daily ad spend is going to look more like a lot of curves rather than a straight line. This is normal for your campaign and it just means that Facebook is going through and optimizing the delivery of your ads to the right market.

You can also choose to work with a lifetime budget. When you do this, you tell Facebook the full amount that you want to spend over the lifetime of your campaign. Then Facebook will divide up the total budget of your campaign, keeping it pretty even across all your campaign dates. You will need to tell Facebook the dates that you want the campaign to go so that the program can average out how much to spend every day.

If you're enjoying this book, I would appreciate it if you went to the place of purchase and left a short positive review. Thank you.

CHAPTER 6: FACEBOOK ADS REPORTING AND OPTIMIZATION

After you took the time to set up your very first ad campaign with the help of Facebook, you can pat yourself on the back. But this doesn't mean that the work is done. While Facebook is set up to do a great job with optimizing your campaigns on its own, you will still need to be on top of things and routinely review if everything is running smoothly. Even if the program does a great job on its own, you will learn what works for your ads and can apply these insights into future campaigns. No matter how amazing the campaign is, you must monitor to make sure that it is performing well.

Looking at Facebook Ads Reporting

The easiest method that you can use to help review your campaign performance is to work with your Facebook Ads Manager. In this program, you will be able to filter your campaigns looking at objectives and dates. You can also zoom in on any campaign to measure the performance of every single ad that you have set up.

When you go through this process, make sure that you have set up the right date range when looking at the ad reports. If you are in the wrong date range, you will look at the wrong information and may be confused about what is working and what isn't. You can also take the time to compare two different ranges of dates. This will help you to compare how your campaign performance is doing over time.

The best way to check how your campaign is doing right now is to look over the past seven days. Make sure to click on this when you look at Facebook Ads Manager. If you go for longer periods of time, it may change all your metrics and can make it hard to understand your recent campaign performance. It won't show how things have changed over time; it will just average everything out. If you want to see these changes, then you will need to compare a few dates together.

As you take a look at your Campaigns tab, you may notice that there are reports for different types of metrics. Some of the options that you can choose include the following:

- Unique link clicks
- Impressions
- Cost per conversion
- Cost per click

This is where you are able to check on the complete overview of all your campaigns on Facebook and how they are performing. You can then select a campaign to look at simply by clicking on the checkbox that is right in front of the campaign name. From here, you can navigate to the Ad Sets and then the Ads tabs. This allows you to see the performance of every campaign unit that you have. The neat thing here is that Facebook is set up to automatically display the data that is the most useful for each campaign.

How to Manage the Ad Report's Columns

While Facebook can do a good job of showing you the most relevant metrics for your advertisement, it is possible for you to go through and change some of the metrics that you see in your ad reports. To do this, you simply need to go to your Columns menu and then select the different reports so you can change your metrics.

From here, you can either select the pre-set reports or you can create some new custom reports. To create a custom report, you just need to click on "Customize Columns" and then click on the reports that you want to create.

One of the best things about Facebook is that you can choose from a wide variety of metrics to add to your report. Some of the most insightful reports that could provide you with the most information on your campaign include:

- Performance
- Clicks
- Engagement
- Messaging
- Media
- Website conversions

- On-Facebook

- Apps

- Offline

After you have had time to create the ad reports that are needed to help you fully understand how the campaign is doing, make sure that you save these reports. This will ensure that you can come back to them later and use them for comparison at a later date. You can also make it so these new reports are your default options.

How to Do Advanced Reporting

In addition to some of the metrics that are shown in the Ads Manager reports we talked about above, you can also take your reports and break them down into even smaller details. These details can make the difference in how you advertise and so much more. The Breakdown menu is going to be your best friend to get this done. Some of the ways that you can break down the reports you have for your campaign include:

- **Delivery**: This could include the time of day, the device, the platform, the browsing platform that was used, the location, gender, and the age.

- **Action**: This could include information such as carousel card, video sound, video view type, destination, and conversion device.

- **Time**: You can pick out the amount of time you want to break down out of the report.

This can be as long as a month or more, and even down to a day.

With the help of campaign breakdown, your business is going to be able to find out the answers to a bunch of questions that can be useful on this campaign as well as on many other campaigns that you come across. Some of the answers that you will get include:

Which of your ad placement choices are performing the best?

What times of the day, or which days of the week, end up giving you the most conversions at the lowest cost?

What are the best-performing target countries?

To break down the ad campaigns by these different criteria, you will need to go into your Ads Manager account and select at least one of your campaigns. It is possible to click on more than one if you wish. You can then go to the Breakdown menu and select the criterion that you want from the list. For example, you could choose to break down the campaign by Placements, which is going to help you to figure out which placements are not doing the best so you can turn them off and not waste time or money.

Take some time to look around the reporting options with your Facebook Ads. There is so much information available here that it can sometimes seem overwhelming at first. After some time, you will have a better understanding of some of the most important ad metrics and which optimization practices are the best for your campaigns.

Chapter 7: Tips to Make Your Facebook Ads Campaign Successful

When you first get started with Facebook Ads, you may be overwhelmed by all the options that are out there for you to explore. Understanding some of the best tips and strategies that are available with Facebook Ads can make all the difference in how successful your campaign is going to be. Let's look at some of these tips so you can get the customers and the sales that you need.

Mine the Insights You Get from Your Audience

One of the best tools that you can use when creating your campaign is Facebook's Audience Insights. This tool is going to help you learn about your audience ahead of time. This can be helpful if you are just getting started on your business. You don't want to spend a lot of money on targeting an audience that you don't know all that much about.

The Facebook Audience Insight tool can help you to mine the data that is available through Facebook. Since there are so many people on the Facebook network, there is a wealth of information on almost any demographic that you can choose. With this information, you will be able to learn exactly who the target market is and what they like or dislike, based on those who are already fans of your business page.

This can be a great tool for a lot of businesses. Instead of just making guesses and hoping that you are right, you can use this Facebook tool to help you know exactly which users are the most likely to follow through on any call-to-action that you place on your ads. It can save a ton of money and time, making it easier for you to focus on the quality of your ad while avoiding wasting any time with your targeting.

Create a Unique Ad Set for Every Audience

One of the features that you can use on Facebook Ads is that you can choose to create different sets of ads for unique audiences. This means that you could effectively create two different campaigns and then deliver them to two different audiences. Or you can create the same ad and then send it out to two types of audiences that are completely different. This basically ensures that you can get better targeting.

Let's look at an example of this. If you are a retailer who sells kitchen supplies, you may have a nice stainless steel bowl that you want to market to two different target audiences. Instead of trying to send out the same ad campaign to each group, you could create two unique ads and then choose where they are delivered. You may have the first ad go to professional chefs and the second one would be towards mothers who stay at home.

Accompany Your Ads with a Landing Page

There are very few instances where you should connect an ad to your product page or your website without first pushing your visitors over to a landing page. These landing pages can be helpful because they will allow you to maximize the efforts that you put into Facebook advertising by educating your users before you decide to get them to purchase from you.

These landing pages can make a lot of sense because advertising on Facebook isn't always cheap. You will need to spend money on all the clicks and to make it cost effective, you want to make sure each of these clicks counts. Simply sending the customer over to a basic product page or website, without providing them with some clear directions on how they should act from here, could be a waste of your money.

Use Imagery That Is Striking

You are going to find entire courses out there on how you can effectively write Facebook ad copy. While the ad copy is really important, you also need to take the time to pay attention to the images that you use in your ads. Visual content is way more influential than your textual content, so you need to pay special attention to that.

The image that you use doesn't necessarily have to be a picture of your service, product, or business. It could be something that is going to catch the attention of your customer and will get them to read the ad. It is best if the picture is relevant to the product, but it doesn't have to match up exactly. Remember that Facebook doesn't want you to have an image that is over 20 percent words, so make sure that your image is there to grab the attention of the customer, not display your message.

Select the Right Placement to Get a Bigger Reach

When you are working on a campaign on Facebook, you can choose from a variety of platforms, devices, and placements. This gives you a lot of choices and a lot of control over your campaign, and the best choice is going to depend on your goals and the type of campaign that you want to create.

One thing that you can try out is to add Instagram to the video view placement, the engagement, and the reach. This can improve your results by as much as 40 percent. However, when you do this, it is likely that you are going to see fewer comments and likes if you are running it as a Facebook page post ad.

You can also use Messenger here. It is a great add-on to traffic and the conversion campaign. Currently, the Messenger ads are going to perform really well.

Audience Network placements are a great way to increase the traffic and reach for your ads in most cases. But you should pay some particular attention to the key metrics that you have. In some cases, you may want to run a campaign on one device because it can lower the amount that you pay. In some niches, Android users may have given you a higher conversion rate while lowering your cost. This is why it is a good idea for you to run a mobile device test in your niche to see whether that would lead to an improvement in your campaign results.

Establish Your Budget and Your Bid Strategy

And finally, you need to make sure that from the beginning you set up a budget and a bid strategy for your campaign. Otherwise, you will keep the campaign going way too long and you will end up spending more than you intended. Facebook has made this part easy though with the use of Optimized CPM.

With this kind of tool, you are giving Facebook the permission it needs to bid for ad space based on any goals or constraints that you provide to it. This is often the best way for you, especially as a beginner, to maximize your budget and avoid any overspending. Until you are able to get an idea of how much the ad space costs, and how to best allocate your budget, just stick with the Optimized CPM to get the most out of your campaign.

Being able to create a great campaign with Facebook Ads can seem a little bit overwhelming in the beginning, but there are so many great things that you can do when you utilize all the features that come with it. While you do need to think about the ad itself, you must make sure you understand the platform that you are using. Once you determine who you're trying to target, and you have a good idea of how much you want to spend on the campaign, then it is easier to focus on some of the smaller details.

CONCLUSION

Thank for making it through to the end of *Book Title*, let's hope it was informative and able to provide you with all of the tools you need to achieve your goals whatever they may be.

Going into the book, we have discussed the number of people using Facebook today, and that Facebook is one of the largest and effective platforms in the social media era for businesses and enterprises. We have discussed the difference between the dashboard options, also known as Overview and the 13 different parts of the <u>Facebook</u> Insights analytics tool.

- Promotion
- Followers
- Likes
- Reach
- Page Views
- Page Previews
- Action on Page
- Post
- Events.
- Videos
- People

- Messages
- A/B Split Testing

All of these topics are important to help you create and run your own Facebook Ads campaign. Make sure to refer back to this book to help you get started with Facebook Ads and bring in customers from today!

INSTAGRAM MARKETING

———— ❧❧❧❧❧ ————

How to Become a Master Influencer & Influence Millions of Followers Using Highly Effective Personal Branding & Digital Networking Strategies

Gary Loomer

TABLE OF CONTENTS

INSTAGRAM MARKETING

INTRODUCTION

Social media has revolutionized how we communicate with one another. Whether you are an individual messaging an old friend or a multinational company trying to engage millions of customers, social media is the conduit through which true, lasting connections are made. These connections are forged through the stories we tell each other - the ideas, the products, the messages we convey. Of all the social media platforms in existence, it is Instagram which both values and fulfils the potential of storytelling. Marketers have known for decades that the power to build an audience, engage with it, and convert a potential customer into a paying one, is best leveraged through such stories, but it is only now with the advent of social media that this form of communication has been democratized for all.

You hold in your hand the guide to Instagram Marketing. If you are a freelancer hoping to reach new clients, an entrepreneur looking to generate interest in a new business, a large corporation expanding your marketing scope, or an individual needing to engage with the general public - Instagram Marketing will make these goals a reality.

In each chapter, we will take you step by step through the most cutting-edge and innovative approaches to Instagram marketing. Both new techniques and tried and tested knowledge will be combined to give you the power to not only reach, but surpass your marketing goals. Each chapter contains a brief introduction of what will be covered for easy reference use and will end with a list of learning outcomes, so you can be certain you have picked up everything you need.

Instagram Marketing is broken down into four parts:

- **Building a Foundation**: An overview of Instagram best practices.

- **Beyond the Basics**: More advanced marketing techniques on Instagram, ensuring you rise above the competition.

- **Monetizing & Marketing**: Ways to leverage your Instagram following in order to create revenue streams.

- **Be Inspired**: Case studies and other inspiring advice from Instagram stars who have already achieved their goals on the platform.

Let us now go on a journey together, so that you can fully realize your marketing potential through Instagram so that you can get your story out there into the world.

PART 1: BUILDING A FOUNDATION

CHAPTER 1: SETTING UP AN EFFECTIVE INSTAGRAM ACCOUNT

I n this chapter, we are going to go through the best practices for setting up an effective Instagram account. If you are a seasoned veteran of Instagram, you should still pay close attention to this chapter, as it may help you identify where you have been going wrong and right.

Preparation is King

An Instagram account has a life of its own. Once it attracts followers, it heads off in a specific direction, hopefully the one you intended! While there are ways to get an Instagram account back on track, if mistakes have been made - we will talk about that in a later chapter - it is always preferential if your account has been built from the ground up with the correct approach.

Preparation is *everything*.

Before signing up for your Instagram account, it is best to have definitive answers to these questions:

- What is my main goal for my Instagram account?

- Which demographic is my Instagram account directed towards?

- Is my Instagram account part of a bigger picture?

- What is my branding?

By answering these questions, you will have a much better chance to establish a successful Instagram account as quickly as possible.

What is my main goal for my Instagram account?

Think of your Instagram as the focal point of a business. What is a business most concerned with? We may not like to think of it in such cold terms, but business success is intimately connected to brand growth and sales. If a business does not focus on these things, then it will slowly diminish until it is no longer viable. However, we need not think about Instagram purely in terms of sales, though monetization as you will see later in this book is an important factor. *You* may have a different goal in mind.

Common Instagram goals include:

1. **Message**: With this goal, your Instagram will be focused on conveying a central idea. This could be a political message. It could also be a personal message, such as an uplifting mantra. Alternatively, it may be a message about a product or service. The concept of message is very important

within Instagram and all social media marketing. If you know the type of message that you want to convey, this will give you a fantastic foundation on which to build your entire Instagram account and campaigns.

2. **Meaning**: You yourself may be searching for meaning in your life. Maybe you are wanting to use your Instagram account to explore aspects of your life and may find that the entire endeavor of having a social media account is purely there for you to discover this meaning yourself. This can be helped with interactions with other users and ideas from other Instagram accounts that you may see. Meaning is not just important in terms of Instagram, it is also a fundamental aspect of life, which must be tended to. For some, Instagram opens up the possibility of exploring this meaning.

3. **Support**: Another Instagram goal could be to use your account as some form of support. Now, what I mean by this is that your Instagram is there to support some other endeavor. Let us say that you have a product that you really believe in and you want to increase its exposure and sales. Instagram is a fantastic way to do this. Perhaps you have a blog, or a book, or a Youtube channel; perhaps even another social media page, which you want to support, Instagram can allow you to do all

these things by funneling people to your desired destination.

4. **Fame**: Last but certainly by no means least, Instagram is undoubtedly a means to achieve a level of fame. Whether that is through travelling or being part of the beauty industry, Instagram is used to generate attention and lasting celebrity. There is no shame in using Instagram in this way, and in fact, if you are looking to establish yourself as a known face or public figure, then Instagram is perhaps the best of all social media through which to achieve this goal.

I want you to think about what your main goal is. Most importantly, I want you to write it down on a piece of paper and keep it nearby whenever you are working on your Instagram account. Open up that piece of paper, look at that goal and understand that your goal must feed into every single post you make. This is the foundation on which everything else you do and on which Instagram relies.

Which demographic is my Instagram account directed towards?

Another key consideration is which demographic you are aiming at. A demographic is simply a slice of an audience. Imagine, if you will, that you restore classic cars. You are using your Instagram account to add much needed exposure to your business. The images you post, as well as your stories, show the beautiful and precise nature of the restoration work you carry out. However, this type of Instagram campaign is not going to be of interest to everyone. It is going to be of interest specifically to only a portion of Instagram users.

But which Instagram users?

Finding out exactly which demographic you should be focusing on will be discussed at a later stage in this book, but for now I want you to have a general idea of who your content is being aimed at. In the above example, it would be people who are interested in old cars and restoration work. More than that, you may also think that the majority of that group will be within a specific age bracket. Just for this example, say that your experience in your business tells you that most of the people who are interested in restoring classic cars are aged 50 and up. This then gives you a great idea of how to target Instagram posts. You know then that you are trying to hit two ideas:

1. Those who are interested in old cars and restoration.

2. People who are aged 50 and up.

These two points then will help you decide how to present your Instagram posts. You will find something called *indirect marketing* (which we will discuss throughout this book) extremely useful and this is a great place to use such an idea. For our car example, you might focus on nostalgic elements of people's lives who are older than 50. Perhaps even some aspects that are not connected to cars, but will move and entice people of that age group to be interested in your Instagram account. You are not directly marketing the cars, but you are bringing in people within the demographic which you feel will be most successful for you.

There are ways to figure out which demographic you should be targeting and again we will discuss this later, but for now it is a good technique to have a general idea for whom your content is intended. You will then be able to cater your content on Instagram for those specific people. Just like figuring out what your main goal is for your Instagram account, the demographic that you are targeting will also inform many of the decisions you make about your Instagram campaigns in the future.

Is my Instagram account part of a bigger picture?

When introducing you to the ideas behind your Instagram account at the start of this chapter, we talked about goals. One of the example goals we gave for an Instagram creator, was the idea that your Instagram account can be used to support a larger framework. That it has a secondary importance. It is not an account just for itself, but rather for your business or your website or some other thing which lives outside of your Instagram account.

Related to this, I want you to think about whether your account is part of a bigger picture not. If it is to promote materials and other content outside of

Instagram, then this will feed into the types of posts you make. You will use something called a call to action (CTA). A call to action is marketing speak for the moment where you want your viewer/customer to make a decision and carry out an action. This can be clicking a link to something outside of your Instagram account.

Perhaps your marketing a discount that you are offering elsewhere. Or maybe you are being paid to post promotional material for a third party and you are providing links for your Instagram followers to click in order to access their products/services. Whichever it is, think about how your Instagram account can be used to filter people through a CTA to content outside of your Instagram profile. This is a huge consideration, especially for those who are monetising their posts, and it is important to highlight this because, again, if you are using your Instagram profile to connect it to materials, content, or products outside of your profile, then this will change the type of posts you are making.

What is my branding?

The final consideration to setting up an effective Instagram account, is understanding branding. Branding refers to the way you present your content so that users:

1. Recognize instantly that the content is yours.

2. Understand implicitly the type of message or product you are selling.

Branding is more than just a watermark, a logo, or a slogan. It incorporates all of these things but also so much more. Your branding is even more important because Instagram is largely a visual medium. That means the colours, the style and the content of your images directly convey messages and meanings to your audience. It is critical that you think about the type of branding that you will have on your Instagram account.

Now, you may already have a solid idea of your branding as you are using your Instagram account to support or link to other endeavors, which already have their own branding. However, you could also be starting from the beginning without a fully formed idea of how to forge the most enticing branding for what you are trying to achieve. Branding is something which, and it cannot be stressed enough, needs to be consistently conveyed. You may find that something does not work quite so well in the beginning, but the worst thing you can do is to constantly chop and change the type of branding you are using on your posts. You want to make sure that you give your branding enough time to breathe and establish itself. Unless you have the best marketing on the planet, it is rare for branding to make a huge impact straightaway. It is an accumulative process, as your followers click on each post; seeing a consistent use of style and imagery to the point that eventually it will instantly connect you to any piece of content which uses that exact same branding.

Branding is intimately connected to the message of your product and the meaning which you want to convey in your posts, so it is an essential part of what you are doing. It also lays the foundation for growth well into the future. If people come to trust your branding or see it as representative of quality, then they are far more likely to be involved in other endeavors or other Instagram campaigns which you carry out, because the branding suggests to them that what you are doing is worthwhile and reliable.

Your branding, then, will affect how you present your material on Instagram. But do not worry, it is difficult to get this right straight off the bat. Instagram pros suggest doing some test campaigns where you post six or seven pieces of content to see what people respond to. Eventually, you may have to tweak or change the branding if it does not work over a longer period, but it is counter productive to do so immediately just because something does not attract success instantaneously.

We will talk more about branding when we are exploring the monetization of Instagram posts later in this book, but it is helpful if you continue to think about the type of branding you are going to use throughout your Instagram career.

Conclusion

We have broadly covered the essential, foundational ideas behind a great, successful Instagram profile. But now we want to deal with the specifics of leveraging these ideas to create Instagram posts which have impact. You should continually reappraise the concepts in this chapter as you are creating your Instagram content and using more advanced techniques. No matter what, you will always be able to whittle down what you are doing to the key components of the message, meaning, support, or fame. Sometimes it will be a combination of these ideas, but you will always be able to use these as an anchor for your Instagram content.

Now we can push on to both basic posting strategies and growing your audience.

CHAPTER 2: BASIC POSTING STRATEGIES

In this chapter, we are going to open the book up and explore basic posting strategies. We will not waste precious time going through a step-by-step process of setting up your Instagram account, this is fairly intuitive and there are many books which deal with such things, but what we are going to do is to establish good, healthy practices on Instagram. Even if you are an experienced veteran on Instagram, you may have picked up bad habits. This chapter then is for those who are just starting out and those who have been using Instagram for a while, but who are open to new ways of doing things.

The good practices in Instagram marketing which you will learn in this chapter, will help you develop social media posts that are both captivating and effective at funneling viewers towards your end goal, as explored in the previous chapter.

Let us get to it!

First Impressions Count

Growing up, you might have been told that it is what is underneath which matters, but in the world of social media first impressions count. That is not to say that your deep meaning or complex message is not important - they are - but these aspects of your Instagram account can only be successful if the first impression you make with an audience member is a positive one. Imagine a situation where all of your Instagram posts are successful, but your latest one conveys a negative image of you or your product. Well, there will be people who will encounter you on Instagram for the first time through that post. Their impression of you will not be a positive one, and therefore you will hurt your brand and lose out on a potential long-time follower. This is also true of your profile overall.

Ask yourself, what is the first thing a new follower will see when clicking on your profile page. They may see a short biography, perhaps a profile picture that you have selected to represent your best side, and a list of your most recent posts. However, in that short introduction of images, recent posts, and bio, you want your followers to have a positive impression of who you are and what they can expect from your Instagram account. This is true of your Instagram posts, which should give potential followers a taste of what to expect from you.

Therefore, you want the first impression to be one which grabs the attention of new and old followers, conveying something about you or a product, and grows your brand recognition by exposing people to your branding.

Slow and Steady Wins the Race

You should be aware of social media burnout as you chart out your posting strategy. Underestimating is one of the biggest and most common mistakes people make online. The relentless posting of content, the stress of feeling that you always have an audience to satisfy. These combine to create a powerfully negative effect on content creators. This is something that you should be aware of. When it comes to posting, regular content is a must, but you need not burn yourself out through the process.

If you post very seldom, however, you cannot expect to grow your audience significantly. If you *do* post far too much, then many of your posts will be overlooked. They will become background noise and your followers may even be annoyed by having to keep up. Slow and steady wins the race. There is a middle ground which you should shoot for which will both grow your Instagram account and protect you from having any sort of personal burnout. Posting once a day works well for many people on Instagram. It allows 24 hours for a post to be seen and even go viral, and it does not necessarily have to take up too much of your time if you have other concerns.

The top brands post on average about 1.5 times each day, so that is about 11 posts per week. If you can keep that schedule going, then you will find it to be beneficial for you. The minimum posting schedule which is effective, is roughly about once every 3 days. The caveat to that is that, if the type of content you post takes much longer to produce, then you have to accept the reality that you will not be able to post regularly, unless it is small updates in between larger projects.

Make it Fun

You might think this goes without saying, but you would be surprised how many Instagram influencers avoid this piece of advice, and at their peril. Your posts should be engaging. Of course, you can cover serious topics, and your brand may be specifically dealing with an area which is difficult to present in a fun way. However, at all times you should try to be entertaining. Boring content will get you nowhere, and in fact it will hurt your brand.

Furthermore, it can be annoying if every second post is a promotional item. Followers want to feel a connection to you through Instagram, and if they feel that they are constantly being bombarded with advertising, then they will feel like they are being used. Make your content fun and engaging by mixing up the type of material that you are posting. Be funny, quirky, and show personality through your posts. This will allow your followers to make a personal connection with you which will then convert them into fans, and even paying customers.

Above all else make your content entertaining, and always remember who your content is intended for. If it is not intended for people with an interest in a specific topic, especially if the topic is controversial, then it may be best to avoid it. Conversely, your audience may thrive on controversy and difficult topics, but you must present these in an entertaining, captivating way.

Live Means Authentic

When Facebook, YouTube and the first generation of social media platforms were developed, content was viewed as pre-recorded as opposed to live. With the advent of Twitch and other live streaming platforms, Instagram, Facebook and other social media sites are now heavily promoting their live streaming capabilities. This is something that as an Instagram user you should embrace in order to be contemporary. Most successful Instagram users make strategic and fun use of the ability to livestream.

Instagram has a fantastic live broadcast feature which has grown to become a full competitor in many ways to YouTube. But it is more than just about being innovative when using live streaming in your Instagram posts. Broadcasting live creates a spontaneous, natural, and authentic experience for your Instagram followers. With so many Instagram images being doctored and enhanced with Photoshop, live broadcasts allow followers to see the real you in hopefully entertaining fashion.

When authenticity means more now than ever in social media circles, it is important to incorporate live broadcasts into your Instagram campaigns. This can take the form of a simple out and about vlog, to question and answer segments which are a great way to engage with your audience. Live streaming is also an effective way to see who your super fans are, the ones who will take the time to watch and engage with you as you go live. This will further help you identify who your key demographic is.

The Power of Disappearing Content

A key component of any interaction between a creator and consumer is one of scarcity. Economic books are filled full of insightful lessons about how scarcity increases demand. Just think of gold and how precious it is to every culture in the world. It is because of its scarcity that it has become precious. This is true of Instagram's story feature. In response to services like Snapchat, Instagram has released a component of its service where you can post to your story timeline. These pieces of content can be images or videos. But the defining feature is that they only last 24 hours after being uploaded. This creates an impetus for your followers to watch and engage with your story before it disappears.

By creating a limited window for one of your stories to be enjoyed, you make your followers feel special, chosen in some way, because they are enjoying content that will no longer be there shortly after. They are privileged, gaining access to something which is a slice of life. One of the great things about the stories feature is that it allows you to post multiple times throughout the day without it flooding your users or blocking your other content posts. However, this does not mean you should post 30 times a day. Instead, posting a handful of times on your story timeline is more than enough on any given day.

Regularly posting to your story creates an intimate connection with your audience, and encourages them to stay up-to-date with your Instagram account, otherwise they would miss out - and no one wants to do that.

Capture Those Captions

The images and videos you post are of course important, but what is often overlooked is the use of captions which accompany them to convey new information. More than that, captions can contain little moments or inspirational thoughts which add value to your visual content, perhaps even explaining the context of said content.

Most importantly, you can include hashtags in your captions for each post you make. Hashtags are incredibly important when it comes to increasing overall engagement with your content. This also allows people who are not aware of your Instagram to find your account through the hashtags that they are following. This could be a wide-ranging topic or a hashtag which is connected to a temporary trend. If you use hashtags which are already in existence, then you have access to a large following, this can be a way to find new audience members. But you can also create your own hashtag and be a leader. Then that hashtag becomes synonymous with your own brand. A combination of both approaches is most useful.

Use Your Users

Your followers can be thought of as consumers or users of the service you are providing. They enjoy what you produce and in return you get to reach one of the main goals that we talked about in chapter 1. However, your followers or users are way more important than just that. You should think of them as the lifeblood of what you are trying to achieve on Instagram. Without a consistent influx of followers who stay with you over time, your Instagram account will stagnate and not reach its full potential.

Continual interaction with your followers, therefore, is a great way to ensure that they continue to follow you. This could be through a number of methods including giveaways and competitions, featuring long-time followers on live streams, question-and-answer posts, and simple responses to comments via text.

One of the most useful ways of leveraging your audience is to employ something called UGC. UGC simply means *user generated content*. By running promotional posts asking for user submissions, you can then use this user generated content to further propel your Instagram account in terms of popularity. A promotion such as this could be asking users to use a hashtag you have developed and make a post under a specific topic linking to your account. You could also then pick the best UGC posts and feature them on your Instagram page, helping them gain exposure to followers themselves. These posts could also be challenge related such as encouraging people to eat a certain kind of food and to take a picture of it, or to reach a specific fitness milestone while running a marathon.

You just have to use your imagination to create a promotional post which is going to bring in user interaction and user submitted posts.

Rinse and Repeat

Whatever your goal is on Instagram, say it is to sell a product, you are not going to maximise your results based on just one post. You will have to make posts about the same product, service, or topic more than once in order to gain the type of traction that you need. This is a rinse and repeat process. However, as we mentioned earlier, you should not flood your followers with constant promotional posts. That means that you have to box clever when it comes to choosing the frequency with which you post about a specific product topic.

There is no hard or fast rule to this; however, posting about such a product or service once per five posts, when you post regularly, is a good place to start. Measure the response you get and if you see followers being annoyed by the promotional posts, loosen it off a little bit and space out the posts to a degree.

Conclusion

In this chapter, we have covered the foundations of basic posting strategies. There are other best practices, but if you look at experienced and successful Instagram posters, you will find that they have based their campaigns on these aspects either deliberately or just through luck. By incorporating and thinking about these aspects each time you post, you will significantly increase the success rate of your Instagram posts and profile in general.

CHAPTER 3: GROWING YOUR AUDIENCE

Now that we have established setting goals for your Instagram profile and a basic foundational strategy for making posts, it is time to look specifically at growing an audience. Growing an audience on Instagram involves meeting three requirements:

1. Enticing people to your posts and profile.

2. Earning followers through this content.

3. Encouraging those followers to become long-term fans and/or paying customers.

In this chapter, we are going to explore these three questions so that you have a good understanding of how to reach the people who are going to propel your Instagram profile towards longevity and success.

Meet Expectations

As with all social media platforms, Instagram has its own posting etiquette. This etiquette arises out of common trends and the way people interact and use the platform. Over time, users become accustomed to the way that Instagram is used and, therefore, they implicitly build expectations about how an Instagram post should look, be formatted and be experienced. We will get to being a *renegade* next and exploring innovative approaches to posting, but especially when you are starting out, posting in a way that users will understand and expect is a good habit to get into.

This includes the way that Instagram is used as a primarily visual medium. It could also be the language that you use, and the hashtags which you employ, along with the layout of your posts. All of these are going to feed into this idea of expectation, providing signposts which you can follow towards producing content which meets the needs of your potential followers. The best thing you can do to learn what these guidelines are, is to find fellow Instagram users who are established within your chosen niche, look at how they are making posts and laying them out, and then emulate this to a degree.

One of the ways you can do this is through the use of filters on your photographs. Images are usually presented in a certain way on Instagram. In a recent study by Iconosquare, which is a service which provides metrics to Instagram users, it was found that there are 10 approaches to the look of an Instagram image which users come to expect.

These are:

1. **No filter**
2. **Clarendon**
3. **Juno**

4. **Lark**

5. **Ludwig**

6. **Gingham**

7. **Valencia**

8. **X-Pro II**

9. **Lo-fi**

10. **Amaro**

By incorporating popular filters into your posts, users will implicitly "get" your content. This is just one example of how you can meet the expectations of Instagram followers.

Break Expectations

Once you have a great feel for the style and layout of posts within your niche and across Instagram generally, you then need to distinguish yourself from the pack. It is important to become a successful Instagram influencer through *differentiation*. To be a leader, not a sheep. By learning the standards and norms of Instagram posts, you should then have a good idea of what you can do differently. In some cases, this will be merely adapting the existing styles slightly, changing them in a subtle way to suit you and your branding.

If you feel like being bolder, then you may wish to completely break from established traditions. It is recommended to do this only once you have been on Instagram for awhile and have really familiarized yourself with the usual way of doing things. Once you master that, then you can include your own expression. This will involve **font choice**, **image content**, **filter use**, the creation of **brand-new hashtags**, and the **innovative planning** of topics to engage with your audience and bring in new followers.

Collaboration

In the early days of YouTube, users soon realised that collaborating with each other was a great way to:

1. Create new content distinct in some way from your usual output.

2. Gain access to another YouTuber's audience.

3. Push yourself creatively and learn new ways of doing things.

4. To lower the burden of content making, sharing it with another person and therefore producing content without having to invest more time.

5. Increase your search rankings.

All of this is true for Instagram. Collaborating is a fantastic way for you to push yourself and learn how to create new forms of content, while in many cases lowering the amount of work you have to do because the workload is shared. The best thing about collaborating is that it is an effective way to network and make friends within your niche. Then when your content is produced on Instagram, those you have networked with in this way will be more inclined to simply share your content organically without being asked.

Cross Promotion

Speaking of gaining access to another Instagram influencer's audience, general cross promotion is always to be encouraged when attempting to grow your Instagram following. The simplest form of cross promotion is simply agreeing to share each other's content.

Cross promotion includes:

1. Agreeing with another influencer to publicly speak about their profile and/or products in a positive way.

2. Exchanging a defined number of promoted posts for each other - if you are paid to do this, you are legally required to include that it is a paid post in the description.

3. Posting links to each other's Instagram profiles on other social media accounts and websites.

4. Leaving comments on each other's profiles and posts.

There are loads of other ways to cross promote. Many of them venture more into the realm of **collaboration**, so combine cross promotion with collaboration whenever possible.

It is advisable to approach a number of Instagram users with a similar following to yourself rather than approaching someone with millions of followers. The reason for this is that it is unlikely the most popular Instagram influencers will want to cross promote with you unless they absolutely love what you are doing. They want to get something out of the cross promotion, and if that does not include either products, money, or being exposed to another significant audience, then they will not feel that it is worth their time. In the beginning, it is best to start small. Once you do some cross promotions with similarly sized Instagram accounts, then you can gauge what is working for you what is not. As your audience grows, you will then be able to offer greater cross promotion ideas to more popular Instagram users.

Use Your Best Times

There is great debate amongst Instagram users with regards to what is the best time to post content. If there was a magical time where most users would be exposed to your content, then everybody would post at that time. That would then probably undermine the whole endeavor because once more your post would get lost in the noise. The truth is, **there is no one size fits all approach to posting at the most popular time.** However, this does not mean that you should not pay attention to when your posts are being most successful.

There is a difference between a general best time for *everyone* on Instagram and the best time for *you* individually. Your individual best time will absolutely exist. In fact, you will probably find that there are a couple of timeframes or windows of opportunity which will work best for you. In order to discover what your best, most fruitful times are when posting content, you need to make several posts and experiment with different time slots systematically. You can measure this through Instagram's own available analytics, which we will explore in a moment, but also through several services online such as Iconosquare, which offers an in depth analysis of your posting habits. You will be able to see which times are most beneficial for you. Target those times and reap the rewards.

See What Works

In the same way that you can monitor which time is most fruitful for you, you can also look to see which types of content are most successful for you. A great way to measure this is both in terms of views and engagement. If people are responding to your content, then you are definitely going in the right direction. At first, you will be able to just eyeball which types of content are working best for you. Over time, however, as you build a long list of posts, it becomes slightly more difficult to analyse what is working best for you.

An effective route to gain detailed access to your statistics and analytics which will show various information about who is interacting with your content, how they are interacting with it, and how often, is to register an <u>Instagram business account</u>. The analytics provided through an Instagram business account will give you valuable insights which are unavailable elsewhere. You will quickly be able to see the type of content which is most popular amongst your followers and what is bringing in new fans.

Once you find out the types of content which are working best for you, rinse and repeat. Keep at it, post similar yet engaging content, and you will build a larger audience.

Ride the Trend

Lastly, you should pay particular attention to trends. Observe the competition, see what people who are interested in your niche are doing and saying and gravitating towards, and then build your Instagram campaigns around this information. There is a concept in marketing known as "alignment". Essentially, all this means is that you see a trend and you align yourself with it. This could be a topic, cause, a product that people are having fun with, or even a way of presenting images and videos to the public.

Trends also can be time specific or connected to definable events. Halloween, Christmas, Thanksgiving and other periods are often hotbeds of activity on Instagram. It is a good idea to develop a plan for these times throughout the year, so that you are not left behind by other people competing in your niche. And it does not need to be a huge celebration, either. It could be International Pirate Day or International Meme Day; whatever it is, try and have fun with it and you will attract followers who are interested in those celebrations and jokes. Alternatively, focus on important causes such as Aids Awareness Day or other such causes which you feel passionate about, and post something related to this on that chosen day.

Conclusion

In this chapter, we have covered a good amount of ideas on how to grow your audience. There are many more techniques out there, so it is a good idea to continue your study in this area. You will also find that certain strategies will work for you better than others. This tends to be specific to your niche and your post content. So, do not be downhearted if one approach does not yield a large number of new followers. You will get there in the end. You just have to believe and try new things. Constantly adapt and never give up.

If you're enjoying this book, I would appreciate it if you went to the place of purchase and left a short positive review. Thank you

PART 2: BEYOND THE BASICS

CHAPTER 4: THE POWER OF STORIES

Storytelling is an ancient art form. It goes back to the beginning of our very species. It is no surprise then that in the 21st-century, storytelling has found new and fertile ground within the medium of social media. Indeed, as we have mentioned, Instagram has its very own method of conveying storytelling to an audience entitled, simply: "Stories".

In this chapter, we are going to discuss the power of stories and how they can be used through Instagram's stories feature to build an audience and extend the overall reach of your Instagram account.

Stories Bring Engagement

Hundreds of millions of people use stories on Instagram each and every day. It was inspired by a Snapchat feature, and allows users to post content such as images and videos which will only last for 24 hours. It is important that you realise that everyone uses them. Businesses, celebrities, and your humble day-to-day Instagram user. As Instagram is owned by Facebook, a similar feature has rolled out on that as well, which allows you to cross post your content which is extremely handy if you have different audiences on each social media account.

Just how powerful are stories? On Instagram, one in five stories on average receive a direct response. That is a powerful statistic of engagement. You cannot afford to overlook the stories feature or you will be left behind by those competing in your space. Some do, because it involves more regular updates and they feel this is not worth their time, but when used strategically, the benefits are impressive. And you need not experience burnout, as stories tend to be short and easy to produce with a lack of polish.

Valuable Stories

While stories are incredibly powerful, this does not mean by simply posting *anything* you will be successful. Like any form of communication on social media, the most successful posts are ones which are thought out and targeted. More than this, stories which work well are the ones which provide *value* to the viewer. If your stories are boring or about nothing in particular, and show no personality, then followers are less likely to continue watching your story feed. It is important then that you keep this idea of value at the centre of every story campaign or post you make. A simple rule of thumb is that if it does not provide value of any kind, do not post it.

But how do you know your post has value? Here are a few elements of value which are worth exploring while you experiment with different posts on your story timeline. Look to expand upon these and you will create value for your followers:

1. **Be a storyteller**: Being a storyteller on Instagram does not mean starting every post with "once upon a time", but it does mean telling a clear and simple story to your audience. Your story, is a collection of ideas and images. A simple story, concisely told, is easier to remember. For this reason, keep your stories pure. Do not clutter them with too many ideas. This is especially true if you have a CTA to which you want your audience to respond. And always prioritise the experience of the viewer. You want your story to have a beginning, middle, and an end, which holds meaning and provides some use to those watching.

2. **Do not be fake**: In the world of Instagram, the manipulation of appearance and character is everywhere. Instagram users continue to present the best possible version of themselves, but they do so in such a way at times which renders the experience sterile. At worst, the person appears inauthentic and fake. To stand out from the crowd these days and to truly engage with people, it is important that you are sincere and believable. It is also important that you are relatable. Your stories then should contain this authenticity. They need not be overly polished or produced. They are a slice of

life, a moment in time which you are sharing from your life, carrying with it a message, pure and simple. Do not strive for perfection, strive to be relatable and easily understood.

3. **Have a point**: As stated above, just because you have a story timeline this does not mean that you should continually bombard it with useless, pointless posts. While it can be charming to simply post a moment from your day, and this will absolutely help your authenticity in doing so; trying to have a central idea behind what your story represents most of the time. Is your post a clip of you buying something in town? Then, be sure to show what you are buying. Just walking down a street quietly looking at the camera is not going to engage your audience. Neither is waffling, unless you are an experienced and talented raconteur. Before you switch your camera on, and certainly before you post, make sure you have a central point to what you are about to capture. Always plan ahead and have a clear CTA at the end of your story if that is its purpose. Remember as well that while we talk about planning ahead, this does not mean that there is no room for spontaneity. Try to add a natural, *real* element to everything you do. Just do so with a point in mind.

4. **Be creative**: As we have established, researching the standard ways of doing things helps you both meet the expectations of Instagram users and understand where you could differentiate yourself from the crowd. When planning out your stories, try to use them in a way that is innovative and different. If that means you are capturing a different type of content from anyone else, fantastic. More than anything, it will probably mean that you are showing your own individuality and individual personality. Think of ways to showcase this, think of your strengths, think of the things that your friends and loved ones love about you and try to show it to the world. This is your individuality. If you have a product you are selling, then likewise, show what you love about that product and why people should get excited about it, why they need it in their lives, but always do so in a creative way. Boredom is the enemy.

Story Ideas

As this book is intended for more intermediate Instagram users, we will assume that you know how to post stories, but if you are unaware how to do this, there are many tutorials available online. You can also find Instagram's own guide on this subject, here. It is a fairly intuitive process. What is not intuitive, however, is how to use the stories feature to reliably grow your audience and improve the reach of your Instagram account.

Thankfully the research is in, and we can highlight several approaches you can use to truly leverage the power of storytelling. These include:

- **Life posts**: These types of story ideas are especially important to individual Instagram users who are their brand. If you are promoting yourself as the brand in which your audience should invest their time and money, then life posts are essential. These can be little video diaries with your thoughts about an issue. Most of the time, they will be posts about the day-to-day things you are doing in your life or the issues you face, however, not presented in a boring way, but rather a charming, informative way. These especially work well when you have not had the time to craft larger more complex stories. Create that personal connection between you and your audience by showing who you are and what your daily experiences are like. Just make sure that this is presented in an interesting, connective way. These types of posts can be videos or images. If you are running a business, this does not mean you cannot make life posts to your company story. In fact you can, and effectively. An example would be focusing on specific individuals within your company and experiences they wish to convey.

- **Tutorials**: Tutorial posts are a great way to increase your audience and provide extensive value through lessons which people can then incorporate in their lives. These tutorials often should be connected to the type of brand you are developing. If you are involved in the beauty industry, for example, then you could make a tutorial about eyeshadow. Likewise, if you are a painter, perhaps you could show a short tutorial about a certain technique that you use. If you are a company which sells computer technology, then a tutorial would work well which shows how to use either your product or another related one. Tutorials add great value and are usually well received by followers, as they are receiving useful information for free.

- **Adventure posts**: These types of posts are similar to life posts in certain ways. They involve more elaborate posts about an activity which you are taking part in, usually a special one-off moment. Alternatively, it could be a location you are going to. Perhaps you are visiting a famous landmark. You could also be abseiling down a cliffside and showing your GoPro footage. But an adventure post does not have to always be so grand. It can also be a story about a trip to the cinema or finding something funny while you are out and about running errands. These adventure posts make viewers feel as though they have a deep connection with you; that they are going on the experience with you. If you are a business rather than presenting individuals as your brand, then likewise you can show people using your product in interesting ways and in interesting locations, or show a staff member who uses your Instagram account going on an adventure of their own to add a personal face to your company.

- **Behind the scenes**: Numerous Instagram users post stories about behind-the-scenes. These are tidbits, images, and videos about the making of your content. If you are a model at a photo shoot, then perhaps you will upload a video showing you at the set. If you are a filmmaker, then perhaps you are showing a behind-the-scenes moment with your actors. Again, behind-the-scenes does not have to be grand. It could be showing your setup in your bedroom that you use to record the vlogs. Behind-the-scenes footage again connects the audience, showing that you are a human being, that you are willing to show your real side, and this brings in authenticity through being less polished than the final product.

- **Deliver news**: Another type of story you could tell involves either commenting or announcing news. Perhaps there is an election on which you will be voting in, or maybe a tragic event which you want to give your opinion on. More removed from the seriousness of real life, maybe your favourite TV show has been cancelled or renewed for a new season and you want to tell people about it. Delivering news to your followers encourages them to comment with their own opinions. Just be wary that in this day and age, the divide between people, especially in terms of politics is huge. So, try to promote a more positive take on things unless a specific political perspective is important to you and your brand.

- **Brand announcements**: If you have any announcement about you, your Instagram account, other social media profiles, or your brand in general, your stories are a great medium through which to keep your followers "in the know". A great technique in achieving this is to pre-empt an official announcement. For example, let us say you are about to launch a new T-shirt, you might show yourself wearing a T-shirt on your story just before making the full, polished Instagram post about it. This again makes your audience feel as though they are closer to you than the ordinary fan, getting the scoop before everyone else. Also, if there are any issues with your brand such as growing complaints about a product/service or issue, then you can quickly address this via a story to minimise the damage before making an official statement.

- **Make lists**: List making is very successful at garnering engagement. You could list your favourite 10 action movies or perhaps your top ten first date dislikes. Whatever it is, you are sure to get people commenting on the entries you have included. They may even post their own top 10 list in response. This works really well at provoking discussion about a topic. Just make sure the topic is interesting, and not about your top 10 favourite socks. Although, that could be funny.

- **Invite a takeover**: Takeovers are a great way to include other creators in your story. You can allow other people to post to your story after vetting the content. You could even announce that your story timeline is going to be taken over by another Instagram user for 24 hours. Alternatively, you could run a competition allowing fans to start posting content to your story. Obviously, providing direct access to your account is not a great idea, so you would have to vet each piece of content before it was uploaded. However, takeovers are fun even for larger companies. You could run a competition asking people to post content about using one of your products in a certain way. Then the winners get to post to your story timeline.

- **Shoutouts**: Lastly, giving regular shoutouts to your most engaging fans, helps forge the impression that you really care about the people who are watching your content. Fans will enjoy seeing that you value them, and this will present a good impression of you to the larger world who may not be aware of you, your product or brand just yet. This helps promote a feeling of community around your Instagram account.

Conclusion

We have covered quite a bit of ground in chapter 4. You have learned the power of stories, how to add value to your stories on Instagram, along with several examples of the types of stories you can post. Using this information, you will be able to build a larger audience and bring in new followers, as well as you show value to your existing fans. Your story timeline is a powerful means to communicate with the world, use it, but do so wisely and with value at its core.

CHAPTER 5: ADVANCED POSTING STRATEGIES

I n this chapter we are going to explore more advanced posting strategies. So far we have established the importance of good housekeeping, basic posting strategies, and leveraging the stories feature on Instagram to fully maximise your return on your content. While all of these combined provide a fantastic foundation for any Instagram account, there is always room to grow. These advanced posting strategies will point you in the direction to expand your approach with new ideas and techniques.

It must always be remembered that your journey as an Instagram creator is a perpetual one, where you must continue the learning process in the continual search of growth and success. Let us now explore a handful of critical advanced posting strategies, which you can use as a basis to continue your Instagram journey.

Connected Campaigns

Connected campaigns are one of the most powerful advanced posting strategies on Instagram. So far, we have focused on your relationships with your followers, taking into consideration the goals which you hope to achieve. These have largely been based on single posts, however, a connected campaign is much broader than that. A connected campaign includes two major components:

1. **Internal content.**

2. **External content.**

Internal content refers to anything which is posted within Instagram. **External content** deals with anything which ties into your Instagram campaign but which is outwith it. An example of an internal piece of content would be an image you post on Instagram, while an example of external content would be a video posted on Facebook about the content of your Instagram image.

Connected campaigns can run for just a few posts or across a longer period with numerous pieces of content. Imagine that you are a games design company using Instagram to promote your latest game. You would probably run a connected campaign with materials such as posters, sneak peaks, and tidbits of information regarding the game you are about to release. These would be posted to your Instagram account and your other social media profiles. You would then move through the release of the game, posting reviews and let's plays from prominent Youtubers. Perhaps those youtubers have Instagram accounts themselves, and you work out a deal with them so that they are posting material about your game, and linking to your Instagram account. This is a great example of using internal content and external content to promote a product. More than that, it shows the beauty of the connected campaign.

What is most important for a connected campaign, is that it contains a **content theme**. When planning a connected campaign, the theme of the content should remain paramount over all else. An example of this would be a series of Instagram posts about recycling plastic. Imagine that this is an issue you feel passionately about, and so you want to post a campaign of posts about this issue. When planning out those posts then, you would be constantly thinking about the theme of those posts.

To strengthen the connective tissue between these posts, you can:

- Link to previous posts with each subsequent release. This allows your users to follow the chain of thought that you're presenting.

- Use a hashtag to curate all that content together.

- Use the same slogan, visual style, or image theme throughout your campaign.

Connected campaigns show that you are developing as an Instagram poster, with a greater understanding of producing content which has value, and is long-lasting. These connected posts could last any amount of time, but it is a very good idea to break the campaign up into quarters and re-evaluate the success of the campaign each quarter. You can then alter your approach or even abandon the campaign before investing more in it if the campaign has not produced the results you are looking for.

Content Calendar

One of the key components of a developing Instagram user, is to take organisational skills seriously. Your posts can no longer be added on a whim. Perhaps you do plan out your posts as we have talked about in previous chapters, but creating something known as a **content calendar** allows you to plan a strategy which extends well into the future.

A content calendar is a blueprint for your entire Instagram approach. It can also include content from any number of other sources including your other social media accounts and websites. Think of it as a map which charts the way for you towards a more successful Instagram account. It is recommended that a content calendar should take into account the next 12 months. This will allow you to plan well in advance for special events such as Christmas or taking a holiday.

Using a content calendar is not just about writing down the posts that you are going to make, it is about seeing the bigger picture about where your content is going. By charting out all of the future posts you are going to make within a defined period, you can see whether you are being deficient in some areas. Perhaps your content is video light, and so you realize you need to focus more on that. Alternatively, your content calendar may show that you are not being as consistent with your releases as you thought. You may also realize that you are investing time in a type of content which is not producing results for you.

Creating a content calendar is fairly simple. You can do it using the calendar function or an app on your computer or mobile device. However, using a service such as Trello is a great way to plan out your calendar function. This provides a number of organizational tools for you, but at its most basic level you will be able to assign post ideas to specific dates. You will also be able to write up lists of potential ideals. This is a great option for working in the cloud if you have a team with you. Each person can then add their thoughts or ideas about your content to the Trello calendar.

Use your content calendar to forge a path ahead and develop a plan of action. Too many Instagram users fall foul of not planning ahead enough. Organization is key, especially as your account grows and you are then dealing with many followers.

Supplementary Apps

Finally, it is important to go one step beyond when crafting your content on Instagram. We talked about the most used filters earlier and how you should familiarize yourself with these to meet the expectations of Instagram users. However, you must also show that you are putting more effort into your Instagram account than many others. You can add more value by staying abridged of other applications and techniques which can differentiate your content.

There are many services and apps which will allow you to create a more unique brand with content specifically designed for your followers. A few of these apps are provided by Instagram themselves. Instagram has developed a few applications which will help you in this area. Three of these are:

1. <u>**Boomerang**</u>: An app designed to make fun moments and capture the unexpected. Much like a GIF, the Boomerang app creates a mini video which can loop back and forward. These videos capture a specific moment and add a level of quirk to your video content. The app also allows you to create compelling video content without investing a lot of time. It essentially captures a burst of 10 photographs from your phone camera and then converts this into a small video. Try to use this in a creative way to add value to your posts.

2. <u>**Layout**</u>: Another app, which Instagram has developed, is the Layout app. This is a great way to remix your content and post an overarching idea in one post. It allows you to combine a bunch of different images in a collage of sorts. You can edit the layout to add your own unique spin to it. This is a great option if you are wanting to showcase a bunch of photographs from the one event or about the one group of people. Again, it

adds value because it goes beyond just a simple image.

3. <u>Hyperlapse</u>: This app allows you to create amazing time-lapse videos. You could show the clouds above rolling past at a fast rate or the stars at night moving together in harmony. You could show the number of people gathering together on a beach for a party moving around and interacting with each other at speed. Or how about the buzzing traffic lights of cars throughout the city streaking across the scene to unknown places. The opportunities are limitless with an app like Hyperlapse.

Conclusion

In this chapter, we have covered a range of more advanced approaches to posting on Instagram. However, this is not an exhaustive list. Continue to expand your knowledge of these new posting approaches. New apps, services, and techniques are developed all the time. Instagram, remember, is a product of technology. As technology continues, you must adapt to it in order to stay relevant and ahead of the curve.

PART 3: MONETIZATION & MARKETING

CHAPTER 6: HOW TO MAKE MONEY ON INSTAGRAM

In this chapter, we are going to explore how you can fully monetize your Instagram account. For many who take their Instagram profile seriously, this is the end goal. If you are an individual person using yourself as your brand, then using Instagram logically leads to you being able to make a good living from your Instagram posts. Likewise, if you are using your Instagram account as promotion for a business or product, you want Instagram to lead directly into sales and other financial opportunities.

With this in mind, let us look then at some of the best ways to make money on Instagram.

Merchandize

Selling merchandize on your Instagram account is a no-brainer. Your own personal merchandize is intimately connected to your brand. It should carry your brand message and style with it. This is the key difference between what is considered merchandize and what is considered an outright product. A product can be used for a specific task, like a blender or car. Merchandize, on the other hand, has been made for one purpose. It carries your brand message with it. Think of someone wearing a T-shirt with their favourite band logo on it. Another example would be a baseball cap with sports team branding on it. Of course, there are places where merchandize and products kind of become the same thing and overlap. For example, Nike produces trainers. People wear those trainers, and those trainers contain the logo for Nike on them for all to see. So in that case, the trainers kind of become both merchandize and a product to be used.

Here are a few merchandising ideas for you to consider for your Instagram account:

1. **T-shirts**
2. **Posters**
3. **Calendars**
4. **Keychains**
5. **Stickers**
6. **Patches**
7. **Pins**
8. **Clothes**
9. **Hats**
10. **Cups**
11. **Bags**

What all these examples have in common is that merchandize carries with it a focus on your brand.

Think of it as a win-win situation. If one of your followers buys some merchandize and then wears and displays it, you get some free advertising into the bargain. What is great about merchandising is that if you are not able to make these items in-house, there are a number of great third-party services such as Teespring which will allow you to quickly produce T-shirts and other items en masse and on demand for your Instagram followers. You can then promote these items via your Instagram account and other social media profiles.

Sell Your Images

Instagram is a visual medium, and so photographs and other images are incredibly important. But they can also be a source of income for an Instagram user. Perhaps you have taken a fantastic picture of an animal in its natural habitat or maybe you have had a photo shoot organized and uploaded. Another example would be capturing an incredible moment incidentally. Whatever it is, these images can be sold.

Options for selling your images include:

1. Uploading for use as stock images via sites such as Shutterstock.

2. Selling your images for use in the press via newspapers, magazines, and news websites.

3. Licence your image for use on promotional materials.

4. Upload your image for use via online printers where people can create their own

bespoke posters, cushions, clothes, and other items.

5. You can also sell your Instagram images directly on websites like Twenty20.

Whenever you do use an image, ensure that you include a disclaimer or contract covering exactly where the image is allowed to be used. This will protect you from the plethora of people and businesses who want to use material for free.

Affiliate Marketing & Sponsored Posts

With affiliate marketing, you make money every time one of your followers clicks a link to check out a product or buy it. With a sponsored post, you are directly paid by a company to promote or review a product. Both can be used to generate significant revenues. Affiliate marketing through companies like Amazon allow you to place a URL (which might not be clickable, which we will discuss later) in your sidebar to a product without even having an agreement specifically with the manufacturer in place. You will then be paid a percentage of the sales from the people who follow that link.

Often as your Instagram page grows, companies will approach you to promote their goods in return for money, a free product, or a discount on something else they are offering. It is down to you to negotiate the terms of these deals. However, you can seek such deals yourself and be partnered with a sponsor through websites such as Sharesale, Ebates, and Stylinity.

Sell a Product or Service

This is going to be especially important for those who are running their Instagram account as part of a business. Selling your products or services through Instagram is a great way to reach new paying customers. You can promote your products by sharing behind-the-scenes information and customer photos. You can also run discounts and other giveaways to increase goodwill towards your brand.

It is a good idea to include a direct link to your product in your profile bio via the website link, and to also include them in your promotional posts where allowed. You can also reach agreements with other Instagram users to promote your services and products. You can do this either by reaching a sponsorship agreement or providing a free product/service for review.

Sell Your Instagram Account

Lastly, you can actually sell your Instagram account. If you build up significant following, you will be able to sell your Instagram brand/account to a third party who will then have access to your followers. You can then walk away to other ventures. An alternative to this, is to sell your account with an agreement that you will still be involved in some capacity as a creative consultant or shareholder.

Believe it or not, there are services which will help you find a buyer for your Instagram account.

Websites such as Fame Swap and Viral Accounts are just two options for those looking to sell or buy Instagram accounts. For some, this is the end goal of their Instagram account; for others they will sell their Instagram account once they feel their brand is in decline. They will then set up a new Instagram account under a new brand and start all over again, but with a substantial amount of money in the bank from the sale of their original Instagram account.

Conclusion

In this chapter, we have covered ways in which you can monetize your Instagram account. Other creative options for monetization do exist, but the above recommendations tend to cover the majority of monetization strategies. By following one of these or a combination of them, it is possible to not only make a living from Instagram, but to also make financial gains well beyond this.

CHAPTER 7: THE SECRET TO SUCCESSFUL ADS AND PROMOTIONS

I n this chapter, we are going to cover the best ways to get the most out of ads and promotions on Instagram. These apply to both promoting yourself and being sponsored. Results will vary, but if you follow the steps taken in this chapter, you will maximize the amount of revenue you can make from ads and promotions, while extending your brand reach.

Linking in Instagram

Whether you are posting about your products or a sponsored product/service, most advertisers will want you to put a link to their products in the description of a post. Unfortunately, at the time of this writing, this can be difficult on Instagram. A quirk of Instagram is that you cannot post *clickable* links in your organic post descriptions unless you have a special type of account. You can, however, post them in your bio as your single website link. But then, why have we mentioned posting links in your sidebar throughout this book? The reason is that there is a difference between:

1. **Standard Instagram posts**

2. **Verified Posts**

In a **standard post**, you cannot include such links in a clickable form, only text. If you have a **verified account**, then you will be able to post such links which can then be clicked. To become verified, however, you will have to have a substantial following. Alternatively, you need to have a business profile as opposed to a personal account and have more than 10,000 followers.

But what about the mere mortals who do not have the ability to get verified yet? Well, there are a few workarounds:

1. **Captions**: Include the link in the caption to your photo or image. It will not be clickable, but your users will be able to copy the link and paste it into their browser.

2. **Another Account**: You can set up another Instagram account through a disposable email address and then include the link you want in the new account's profile. When you post your image or video, you can then put the name of that account in the post. It will be clickable. People will click on it and will be taken to the profile of that other account. It is messy, but will get people to the link you want them to click.

With these workarounds in place, you will be able to more successfully place affiliate links and links to your own adverts through your content.

Secrets to Running Effective Ads

If you are going to run your own adverts and promote your own products/merchandize, then it is essential that you understand some basic advertising techniques which will boost your effectiveness. You can also apply these to offering a better advertising strategy to third parties as well, if they do not provide you with specific advertising guidelines.

These include:

1. Having a clear message.

2. Having a concise message which is easily understood without your audience having to jump through any hoops.

3. Having a branded message which can be instantly connected to you and your products.

4. Targeting your audience demographic through paid ads.

5. Designing your adverts with a demographic in mind, stylistically creating something which will resonate with them on both an aesthetic and symbolic level.

6. Create adverts which are captivating visually.

7. Do not over saturate with repeat postings.

8. Listen to audience feedback.

How to Promote Successfully

Promoting something via affiliate marketing or sponsorship on Instagram requires a bespoke approach which is appropriate to the product, service, or individual you are marketing. However, there are some specific lessons which can be applied to promotion on Instagram, which will increase the likelihood that your approach will be successful.

When formulating your plan, keep the following in mind:

- **Positive Association**: Psychology plays a huge part in any type of advertising. If an advertiser has contacted you and asked you to promote their product or service, they understand that already. It is down to you to take advantage of this psychological aspect and be persuasive. Positive Association is a huge part of this. Try to present the positive side of what you are promoting. Your followers will only buy a product if associated with a positive experience. Keep your criticisms then to a minimum.

- **High Energy**: As well as being positive about a promoted item, you should try and remain high-energy when presenting it. The 18 to 35-year-old demographic which most advertisers are interested in, implicitly expects enthusiasm about the product. You can be as positive about a product as possible, but if you present that in a low-energy way, people will not be interested in what you have to say.

- **Captivate:** The advertising you make for a product or service needs to be captivating.

There are two aspects to being captivating. The first is to catch the eye and the second is to hold the attention. Think about these two things when designing your approach. You want something that followers are going to be immediately interested in, but you want to present it in such a way that they will not get bored.

- **Engage:** Lastly, if you are unable to engage your audience then advertiser paid promotions will surely dry up. Advertisers want to see a real return on the paid posts you have provided. Engagement is the way to make sure that the promotions you run, work. And by engagement, we are talking about your followers taking an action in some capacity like the CTAs we mentioned earlier. This could be with a comment or a like. Ideally, it will be following a link to a paid product and then making a purchasing decision. When advertisers see that you are able to persuade your followers to purchase goods in this way, many more of them will come forward with promotional opportunities. Think about engagement, think about funneling your followers towards buying a product. If this is at the core of your approach, any advertising promotion will be successful. This applies to promoting both your own brand and the products/services of a third party.

Be Wary

Be very wary when entering into advertising. Your brand is a lasting thing, and to ensure its success you have to be trusted. This is true of Instagram more than any other platform on the planet. The connection between you and your followers means something. If your followers feel that you have betrayed their trust, they will abandon you swiftly. In other words, do not promote a product which is extremely flawed at best, or worst, is seen as some sort of misleading scam. It does not matter how much money you are offered, your brand and your success in the future demands that you promote ethically to your followers. To avoid these problems, ask to try out any service or product that you are promoting. Get used to it, and think about how others will react when they buy that product/service.

Conclusion

In this chapter, we have covered the secrets behind running successful ads and promotions. These can be applied to your own promotions and sponsored deals. Stay ethical, stay positive, at all times keep your eyes open when promoting. If you do that and drive your followers towards engagement, you will continue to be successful both as an Instagram user and a promoter of third-party goods.

If you're enjoying this book, I would appreciate it if you went to the place of purchase and left a short positive review. Thank you

PART 4: BE INSPIRED

CHAPTER 8: THE MINDSET OF AN INSTAGRAM STAR

N ow that you have a great idea of how to run a successful Instagram account and how to grow it, the one final ingredient is mindset. Why are some Instagram users successful and yet others are not? Is it the case that some people just have talent and others do not? Are those of us who do not have success damned to accept failure? Of course not! The difference between a successful Instagram user and an unsuccessful one can be boiled down to having the **right mindset**. In this chapter we are going to briefly look at the type of mindset you need to become an Instagram star.

Looking at all of the successful Instagram users, you will see traits which are shared between them all. Sure, there will be the odd person who has simply found success through sheer luck. But, the majority of Instagram users who are successful, have done so by relying on, or cultivating, certain approaches to success. These can be boiled down to four main characteristics:

1. **Passion**

2. **Discipline**

3. **Hard Work**

4. Study

We will now look at each of these. As you read about them, be honest about yourself. Which characteristics do you possess? And if you do not possess one or more of these, do not feel downhearted, instead persevere and move forward to cultivate these characteristics within yourself.

Passion

To be a success and to combine this with longevity requires passion. A drive towards something which you truly care about. It is contagious to be around someone who is filled with passion for what they are doing. It is one of the reasons why people watch Instagram users and Youtubers. That level of passion is infectious and makes us feel more alive. But it does more than that when you are an Instagram user. Passion is what gets you through difficult times. When things are not quite going your way, it is passion which provides you with comfort. There is still an enjoyment in what you are doing. A love for it. If you have a love for the brand, product/service, or idea you are trying to convey through Instagram, then nothing can stand in your way. You will attract people to you because passion is addictive. It pushes on and gives us the energy to achieve, and it is something that people like to be around.

Discipline

But despite the passion which we may have, it is discipline which truly makes us endure. You will often hear people talking about trying to find inspiration. Or rather, they will wait for it to appear. Writers often talk about having writer's block. However, it is not true that you have to wait to push through these times. What you truly require is discipline. The ability to sit down regularly and get the work done. Discipline is what gives us the ability to organize and plan. These are two critical talents when creating an Instagram account which will resonate with people. Content plans do not just appear out of the ether. When we do not feel like working, it is discipline which tells us we *must*. It is discipline which gets us to at least start and try when we feel tired. And so cultivate discipline, you will find that every successful Instagram user who posts consistently, does so because discipline gets them through when they cannot be bothered to post.

Hard Work

Attached to discipline is the idea of hard work. Instagram users often look as though they are effortlessly living and producing first-class content. But this is not true. It is hard work which produces results. If you think being an Instagram user is not going to be difficult or does not require effort, then you will fail. Being an Instagram star is not about avoiding work, it is about embracing work which we need to do in order to make things happen.

Work which enriches our lives both financially and emotionally. Be prepared to work hard. Roll up your sleeves and get stuck into your content plan. With hard work, you will scale the mountain. Without it, you will continue to look up at the peak and wonder what could have been.

Study

Finally, study is an essential part of the Instagram star mindset. All the people who are successful on Instagram stay abridged of technological changes and trends which they must be aware of. The last thing you want for your brand is to appear irrelevant and out of touch. And so, you must continue to study new ways to market yourself; along with what your competitors are doing, new changes being made to Instagram as a service, and any new applications which may make your profile more successful. Always be a student. Always learn. And always take this new knowledge forward with you, using it in a way which is innovative and inspirational.

Conclusion

In this chapter, we have covered the four main aspects of the winning Instagram mentality. The mentality which separates those who are successful on Instagram from those who are unsuccessful. As I mentioned at the beginning of this chapter, if you feel you are lacking in any of these four areas, then take that as a positive thing. Use it as an opportunity to open yourself up to learn more. Drive yourself forward with the commitment that you are going to take on these mindsets. At first, it will be difficult. All habits are. But after just a few weeks, you will notice a huge change in who you are. You will have gone from someone who is lost, to someone who is passionately and purposefully moving towards an achievable goal. The goal of being a true Instagram star.

Chapter 9: Inspirational Instagram Success Stories

In this chapter, we are going to look at inspirational success stories. These are success stories which you can turn to in times when things are perhaps not going your way. Remember that all the people who have had successes on Instagram at one time were failing. The following three inspirational accounts are there to show you that being a success on Instagram, more than anything else, is about staying the course.

An Eye For Success

In 2013, Chris Buckard had not yet experienced success as a photographer. At least, he had not reached his potential. It was Instagram which provided this potential. At that time, he was travelling, trying to make his living photographing the world around him. But when he was introduced to Instagram by a friend, his world eventually changed. He started out humbly, sharing the photographs which he had taken on his travels. It took some time to gain traction, but that decision to start sharing photographs on Instagram changed Chris Buckard's life forever. At the time of this writing, he has over 3.4 million followers on Instagram. It has become a bit of a career in of itself. His secret was people valued the content he was producing - the beautiful photographs which captured the incredible vistas and amazing moments for his followers to enjoy. Because he maintained that same dedication to quality, his posts resonated with people. That in turn, brought in an audience. Remember this, when things are not going according to plan. Brilliant success may be just around the corner, and you are not even aware of it.

Dressed to Thrill

Anish Bhatt is one of the most inspirational people on Instagram. At the time of this writing, he has around 1.7million followers. But he was not always that successful. In his late 20s, Anish was facing personal ruin. He had been fired from his job and the road ahead was dark and uncertain. He was forced to abandon the life he had tried to make for himself and head back home to his parents. But what he did next, changed his life forever. Anish leveraged the talents he had. He had learned a lot about fashion design and photography. He then combined this with his passion for watches, and began taking stunning pictures related to this, sharing them on Instagram. While advertising is important, it costs money. This is something Anish did not have. It is incredible that he reached well over 1 million fans in a purely organic way without ever paying for an advert. He was interested in other Instagram users and their passions. He connected with people, he engaged with those around him on Instagram. And then he put himself at the centre of his brand. Now, instead of marketing watches and fashion, he markets himself. This has taken him to Monaco, London, and Dubai. He is a true jet setter, and it is all thanks to Instagram. His dreams were made possible because they grew out of the ruins of his previous life. Social media can do that, it can turn the darkest moments of our lives into stories of joy and abundance.

A Good Mood

Many turn to Instagram for motivational help. Jason Stone is one of the most successful people who has harnessed this area within Instagram. By using his Instagram account to convey positive thinking and inspirational moments, the world has been captivated by his account. Not only that, but what started out as a drive of passion has quickly turned into a lucrative business with numerous passive revenue streams. Generating more than a hundred thousand dollars a month, he does this without investing in any advertising. But what Jason did next, should prove even more inspirational to entrepreneurs. He took one type of Instagram account and then used it to open up another door in his life. He created a business which offers low-cost advertising to smaller businesses. He generated the momentum to build that business into a huge franchize with millions of dollars. The business, known as Door Coupons, has expanded to many countries across the globe already. It continues to grow and is an excellent example of how one person can use their personality and positivity to then monetize their content through business investment. Jason Stone is just one individual who has achieved this, but there are many more. If you are hoping to break out into many different business fields and beyond, then this is one story which is worth holding onto as a guide.

Conclusion

The point of these stories is to motivate you. It is to help you see that people do not always start with success. What Instagram offers more than anything else is beautiful uncertainty. The success which comes with Instagram opens new doors. It channels your energies into unseen, unpredictable positive avenues. Just by posting images and videos on the Internet, you are able to generate, not just an income, but an entire way of life which will positively affect all your loved ones and even millions of strangers around the globe. Return to these stories and study other success stories as you encounter them. There are things to be learned there, and in your darker times when things are not quite going your way, you will feel motivated by the fact that these successful people were once in your exact circumstances, and then prevailed.

AFTERWORD

This book is only the beginning of your Instagram journey. It is a blueprint to a better future. A way to reach your goals. Build on what you have learned through these chapters. Continue to be a student of **trends** and **innovation**. Cultivate the correct approach of the **Instagram star mindset**. Continue along your journey and never be afraid to alter your approach when things are not working as you had hoped. Instagram is a competitive place, but if you **leverage your individuality** in everything you do, then you will have a great chance at success. Because Instagram is about celebrating individuality of people, products, and businesses. By celebrating your uniqueness, you can give something to the world that no one else can - **you**.

If you enjoyed this book, I would appreciate it if you went to the place of purchase and left a short positive review. Thank you